WORK
AND
REWARDS

WORK AND REWARDS

Redefining
Our
Work-Life Reality

William F. Roth, Jr.

New York
Westport, Connecticut
London

Library of Congress Cataloging-in-Publication Data

Roth, William F.
    Work and rewards : redefining our work-life reality / William F.
  Roth, Jr.
      p. cm.
    Bibliography: p.
    ISBN 0-275-93166-8
    1. Job satisfaction. 2. Job enrichment. 3. Work and family.
  I. Title.
  HF5549.5.J63R62   1989
  306'.36—dc19   88-25572

Library of Congress Catalog Card Number: 88-25572
ISBN: 0-275-93166-8

First published in 1989

Praeger Publishers, One Madison Avenue, New York, NY 10010
A division of Greenwood Press, Inc.

Printed in the United States of America

∞

The paper used in this book complies with the
Permanent Paper Standard issued by the National
Information Standards Organization (Z39.48–1984).

10 9 8 7 6 5 4 3 2 1

This book is dedicated to my wife,
Wendy, to our two young sons, Ian
and Dane, and to all the other
children whose work life reality
we are currently helping to redefine.
May we remember them well as we go
about our task.

CONTENTS

PREFACE

During my years as a corporate consultant two things have become increasingly obvious to me. The first is that a vast majority of employees on all levels and in most businesses are not satisfied with their working lives, or with their lives in general. In the board room, in front of bosses, in front of direct reports everything is great. Later, however, over a martini or two, or a beer or two, what comes out is totally predictable. They are tired of the repetition found in most jobs, the meaningless busy work, the back stabbing and conflict. They are tired of unpredictable bosses, tired of trying to keep up, tired of not being able to spend enough time with their families, tired of wasting their potential as both employees and individuals. In essence, they feel that things are not what they should be, not what they could be, and they are frustrated.

The second thing that has become increasingly obvious is that, despite their frustration, most employees have been forced to accept this situation pretty much as an unavoidable part of their existence. They worry about it, they gripe about it, but they don't seem to be able to do much to change it.

One of the key factors contributing to our inability to move in the right direction, in my opinion, is our lack of an appropriate framework into which to fit the pieces. More specifically, the key definitions upon which our current work-related perspective is built—those of "work" itself, of the role of "technology," of "rewards," of employee "development," and of "success"—are outdated. Most of them, in fact, are leftovers from the 16th century. Until we update them, until we rework them and fit them together in a more appropriate manner, progress will remain difficult, for they are the foundation blocks upon which our workplace culture is built.

This, then, is the purpose of *Work and Rewards*, to help develop 20th-century definitions for these building blocks. The book's second objective is to show what is possible, both in our work lives and in our lives in general, once the perspective spawned by this new framework is accepted.

The above challenge has been both interesting and difficult. I could not have met it without a lot of assistance. First, I would like to thank the Wharton School professors who taught me to think systemically, who helped me to develop the world view necessary to write a book of this sort. They are Russell Ackoff, Eric Trist, Hasan Ozbekhan, Jamshid Gharajedaghi, and Fred Emery.

Also, I would like to thank my Uncle, Fred Roth, whose on-going research provided me with a significant portion of my support materials and whose continual encouragement has been deeply appreciated. I would like to thank Eileen Tasca and John Kalish, good friends and two of my chief advisors on all projects. I would like to thank Henry Argento, who never let me doubt for a minute that I could do it if I was willing to make the necessary effort. Finally, I would like to thank Caroline Trist, who read the manuscript at a critical juncture and helped me to get back on track.

Part I

THE WORLD WE LIVE IN

"Our time is a time for crossing barriers, for erasing old categories—for probing around. When two seemingly disparate elements are imaginatively poised, put into apposition in new and unique ways, startling discoveries often result."

—Marshall McLuhan
The Medium Is the Massage

1

TO HAVE AND HAVE NOT

BRIAN

Brian rides the New Haven line down to his job in New York City every weekday that he's not away on a business trip. He rises at 6:00 A.M., trying to catch the alarm before it jangles to life, and slides out of bed so as not to wake his wife, Cathy, and two-year-old son, Eddy, who has climbed in maybe an hour earlier and lies with his arm around Brian's neck. Sometimes the child awakens and whimpers, "Daddy, don't go," hanging on until Brian gently pries him loose, promising that he'll come home that night, or maybe in three days.

Brian showers rapidly and does 20 situps, 20 pushups. Everything is in place, his suit hung out the night before, his wallet, watch, and keys on the dresser top. Cathy usually comes downstairs as he drinks coffee and pokes half-heartedly at a bowl of granola. If he hurries he can catch the 6:55. He'd rather wait for the 7:13, but trains have been running late recently and he has an important meeting with his boss at 9:00. He pecks Cathy on the lips, pats his dog, Jessy, on the head, and rushes from the house to his car in the early morning grey. He speeds numbly to the parking lot, running one light.

At the station everyone is in a hurry. An irritated horn blares as he crosses to the stationhouse. Very few people look at each other or speak. Brian enters the old brick building, where once a month he waits in line to pay $145 for his commuter pass, and buys a *Wall Street Journal*. He moves out onto the platform if it isn't too cold and buys more coffee and a cream-filled doughnut at the concession. He pauses briefly to worry about the growing ribbon of fat around his middle before bolting the doughnut down and hurrying to his chosen end of the platform to join a small cluster of commuters standing where the doors to the first "no smoking" car will open. Four years ago, when he was new to the scene, he had smiled and said "Hello" or "Good morning." Very few commuters had replied. Now he just stands silently, huddled inward, isolated amongst the familiar but unresponsive faces.

Once aboard, Brian habitually turns right, moves to the second or third triple-seated row and sits on the aisle so that if he's working on a report his writing arm is free. As the train moves toward New York a few passengers doze. The majority read their *Wall Street Journal* or *New York Times*. Several read the *New York Post*, *U.S.A. Today*, or a paperback. Some do office work, a few regulars play cards, and a very few carry on conversations. One small group of conversant men and women in particular has always attracted Brian's attention. He calls them the "chicken coop." They board his car daily and sit just beyond the door on his side in the two rows of seats facing each other, chattering gaily all the way into New York City. They rarely miss a day. A lot of people avoid them. Some, including Brian, try to sit close.

Other than the chicken coop, Brian rarely hears much noise beyond the muffled clatter of train wheels. Most people who speak do so quietly and without enthusiasm. Brian once read a baseball fantasy on the train. He had frequently laughed out loud, drawn into the book's light-hearted warmth. One morning when he laughed, a young executive in a dark grey pin-striped suit, silver-rimmed glasses, and ebony-black hair swept straight back had turned in the seat ahead to scowl briefly. When Brian laughed again the young man had cringed, as though being hit, and others had stirred uneasily.

Usually he had found a seat, but on some days he was too slow and was forced to stand for most of the one hour and 20 minute ride, his feet and legs aching. Brian was beginning to worry about his legs. He hadn't been able to run regularly for almost two years now. Eventually he had signed up for use of the company gym, but was still 43rd on the waiting list. Even if he gained access, however, he didn't know when he would be able to take advantage of the facility. During lunchtime it was crowded. Using it before work would mean rising at five instead of six. Using it after work would mean arriving home at eight instead of seven. He ran some on weekends, but usually had to work on the house, in the yard, or was too tired. His body was going downhill due to lack of exercise, and he could see no way to improve his situation.

Brian was doing well with the company. He was considered a "comer." He worked hard and knew that people were noticing him. He made a good salary and has his own office on the 40th floor of a building in the center of Manhattan. From his window he could see the Statue of Liberty in the harbor. He owned a medium-sized, split-level house with a larger than usual lawn in a prestigious, upper-class, New England town. He had two nice cars. His children would be able to attend private school. He shared his secretary with only one other person and told jokes well.

For some reason, however, Brian suspected that he wasn't really satisfied. He was successful. So far he was doing exactly what he had set out to do. But something was missing. At the office there was the constant competition, the jockeying for an advantage, for exposure to people from the 46th floor. But he was used to that. Brian understood the game and knew how to protect himself. But there was always tension. Who was up to what? Who was getting a little ahead? Also, there was the strain of knowing that he might be transferred at any time if somebody upstairs decided it was beneficial. He would leave the company if they tried to transfer him, unless the package they offered him was too good to resist.

They could also riff him. Brian didn't want to think about that. Even though he was doing a good job, no one was safe. The company was very large and traditional. Vice presidents and directors tended to build empires. Periodically, when times got hard or a new CEO came in, there were mass layoffs. During the last one, 20 percent of the people in his division had been axed, all in three days. Brian had survived, but he would never forget the dazed look on the faces of the older men and women wandering numbly around the office and halls, men and women who had been with the company for a long time, who probably would have trouble finding other positions, men and women who had done a good job.

On the bright side of things, a lot of people he worked with were friends. There was camraderie and respect. Brian looked forward to Tim popping into his office with the latest news; Florence bringing flowers into the conference room to brighten it up; trading tips on child rearing with Mary, his secretary; Joe's endless stream of "trivial pursuit" questions. He got along with just about everyone. The one major exception was the type of individual he had labeled "politician." Brian hated the politicians. He had found them everywhere he had worked. Here it was Melissa Tanner. The politicians spent their time manipulating people. They were qualified to do little else. They wanted to know everything that was going on, everyone's opinion, and had no qualms about reshaping this information in whatever way they perceived to be advantageous to their careers. They had no scruples whatsoever. Their only objective was to win, no matter what the cost to others.

Melissa, however, was not responsible for the growing uneasiness in Brian's gut. His work had become his life. Everything revolved around it. He was not against work. He wanted and needed his job, not only because it paid the bills, but because of the respect it earned him. Still, there had to be more. He was usually tired. He had been tired now for more than a year. He rarely caught up with his project work. He had never really figured out how all the pieces fit together and was beginning to wonder if anyone else had. Often he didn't understand the usefulness of the projects and policy changes those above kept piling on him. He simply did what he was told, worrying less and less as time went on about the meaningfulness of his efforts. It was a numbness. On the outside he was sharp, saying the right things, keeping his ear to the ground. But on the inside he felt numb and increasingly bitter.

He had joined the corporate world eager to learn, to contribute, to prove himself. But every time he had come up with a good idea, an innovation, or improvement, he had bumped into someone, trespassed on someone's territory, threatened someone, and been shoved back into line, sometimes quite roughly. After losing one job partially because of such an intrusion, he had learned his lesson. He had learned that no matter how much he hated them, it was the politicians who did well in the corporate world, more so than people with ideas. The trick was to identify the person who could help your career the most and get your nose as close to his or her butt as possible. The second trick was not to make waves. The competition was already too fierce without giving it an opening. Survival was the key objective, rather than making a contribution.

So Brian had become a survivor. He had carefully mapped out his territory and patrolled the perimeters endlessly, bristling whenever he discovered a strange footprint in the sand. He had picked out his champions and courted them constantly. He had learned to set his projects up so that he could take credit for good results and shift the blame for bad ones. He had refrained from making radical suggestions.

Though he didn't like to admit it, the strain of work was affecting his family life as well. He didn't know Eddy very well. He had been away on a business trip when his son was born. He saw maybe an hour or two of the boy on weekday evenings. "Quality time" they called it, but that was crap, too. Both of them were worn out by then. Frequently the sessions ended up with Eddy doing something he was told not to do in order to gain Brian's full attention, Brian losing his temper, Eddy running to his mother crying, and Brian left feeling frustrated and guilty. It was pretty obvious that the kid needed a lot of time, a lot of patience, a lot of encouragement, and Brian wasn't giving it. And now Cathy was pregnant again and there would be even less time for Eddy. Cathy seemed to be drifting away, too. Her world was increasingly different from his. She frequently asked what was going on at the office and listened patiently while he tried to explain, but Brian knew that she wasn't really interested, that it didn't have much meaning for her out here in suburbia.

He had tried to talk to friends at work about his growing sense of alienation from his family. They hadn't been much help. "Just the way things are," they had shrugged. "Success takes sacrifice, you know that. You have to be willing to make tradeoffs." They all had made tradeoffs, frequently painful ones, he had discovered. Work was all that some of his older confidants had left in their lives.

Brian had begun to suspect that something very basic was out of whack. The term "success" had somehow been perverted. He had been led to believe that "success" ensured the good life. It didn't. Something important was missing from the definition. He had eventually realized as he sat staring out the window one morning at the world whizzing by that he felt betrayed. He had done everything that he was supposed to do, and it wasn't working. He had made all the right moves, gained all the right credentials, but that didn't seem to be enough. Or maybe the constant pressure was getting to him, maybe he was just confused. That thought scared him terribly. His monthly mortgage payment was $1,147, his car payment approximately $240. They needed a new oil heater; their old one gulped down several hundred dollars worth of fuel a month and could give up on them any day. Eddy was starting nursery school next year, and the new child was due around Christmas. Cathy was already thinking about a new house with another bedroom. She also wanted to get on with her career. Cathy wasn't as excited about the second pregnancy as she had been about the first and had been talking about bringing in a nurse or au-pair almost immediately to take care of the child. That would be another expense.

Brian sighed. Tomorrow he was flying out to the new plant in Chicago to help organize a design process. Maybe he would be able to begin sorting all this out on the plane, though his report on staffing levels was due next Monday and he should work on it. Maybe next week, while commuting. But where would he start? What would he change? He had read about people walking out of their offices one day and never coming back. Instead, they had opened a small restaurant somewhere, or a hobby shop, or learned a craft, or done some consulting. The stories had excited him. If he were to make such a move he had decided that his next occupation would be one that left him a lot of free time. He had always wanted to learn French. He had vacationed in France once and had fallen in love with the language. Also, he would take up sailing. Maybe he and Eddy could learn to sail together. He would read the stack of books sitting on his desk and start playing tennis, get his legs back into shape. The first thing he would do, however, would be to take a long, relaxed trip with the family, get to know them again.

Brian leaned his forehead against the coolness of the train window. Nice dreams, but all those things took money. Practically, he knew that he couldn't possibly afford such a move for a long time to come, probably never. It was too big a financial risk. The only real chance he saw was that maybe as he rose through the corporate ranks and gained increased control over his situation he would be able to relax more, enjoy life more. At least he hoped that he would. But the kids would probably be in school by then, have lives of their own. He closed his eyes and sighed again. This time it was a sigh of unwanted resignation. The long train ride in the dull, grey morning sometimes seemed endless. It was slowly beginning to symbolize his life, though he could not believe that somehow there wasn't more. . . .

SHARON

Sharon is a secretary with word processing responsibilities. She had started as a typist but realized quickly that the typewriter was on the way out and had signed up for a word processing course in the evenings. She had been right. Most of the women who had lacked the time, money, or inclination to take similar courses were gone. Now she was studying a computer language. Her boss had told her it would be a wise thing to do in terms of her career.

During office hours, however, Sharon currently spent most of her time sitting in front of a terminal screen, entering new documents or making changes in old ones. It wasn't especially difficult work. She rarely understood what she was copying onto the disks. She just punched the right keys and let her mind wander. She was good enough by now that she didn't have to pay attention. While working she switched onto automatic and became part of the terminal, but a part that had to stretch and move around occasionally to get the circulation going again. She used to listen to a small radio, but that had been ruled out as a distraction. The worst thing about the job was the isolation. It was lonely sitting there by yourself staring at a screen most of the day. She had gotten into the habit of calling her mother occasionally, or Nancy, or Theresa. The company frowned on personal calls during working hours, but everyone did it. Life had to go on. There had to be more than the word processor. Anyway, she could type while she was talking.

Sharon still had other duties as well. She was responsible to a department director. The secretarial staff had been cut by almost 40 percent since Sharon began with the company. It was rumored that even more cuts were coming next fall. So now she unofficially took care of two staff managers as well as her director, although "taking care of" no longer meant what it used to. With her first boss, Bob, she had sat in on meetings to take notes; she had huddled with him every morning to schedule the day's activities; she had frequently taken care of personal chores, like remembering his daughter's birthday and helping him pick out a gift. She had known what was going on in the department. She had been a focal point, a nerve center, coordinating projects with other secretaries, making the system work.

All that was changing now. Her current boss, Dorothy, put the daily schedule of activities on her DVX for the entire staff to listen to. Meetings were frequently taped, the tapes edited before coming to her. Sometimes her bosses didn't speak to her directly for several days at a time. She still had contact with other secretaries in the department, but there wasn't as much. The secretaries used to have a well-developed network, keeping each other informed as to what was happening, which of the bosses were good to work with, which were not, which of the bosses were on the way up, which drank too much at lunch, who were having affairs with whom. The network still existed, but it wasn't the same. For one thing, almost all of the people she had started with 12 years ago were gone. She was considered the old timer on the floor.

Despite the changes, Sharon's situation was about as good as she could hope for. She was earning a decent salary. The benefit package was respectable. The company was paying for her computer course. As far as she knew, they weren't planning to lay her off. But life at the office wasn't as enjoyable and interesting as it used to be. The tension level seemed to be climbing steadily. A memo had recently come down after consultants had completed a time-motion study recommending that support staff be "encouraged" to pack a lunch, or to bring something back from the cafeteria and eat it at their individual stations. Before, when the load was heavy, Sharon had sometimes skipped lunch entirely, or somebody had brought it in for the whole staff. Other times, when nothing was happening, she had taken an extra 15 minutes. It had evened out. Now, however, the objective seemed to be making sure that everyone stayed at their desks and at least looked busy from nine o'clock to five, whether or not they had anything of value to do.

The main problem was that work wasn't "fun" anymore. The drudgery had been bearable so long as she had been able to laugh and gripe about it with others in the same situation. Now, however, there was very little to look forward to besides her paycheck as a reward for spending eight hours a day, five days a week in the office.

Jake, her husband, felt the same way. He worked with an automobile parts manufacturing company. He had been there 18 years now. He had started out sweeping floors and hauling out rubbish. He had worked his way up—an assistant machine operator, a machine operator, then maintenance for a while. He had made foreman four years ago. He knew everything there was to know about the machines. He could tear one down and put it back together again blindfolded. But now they were beginning to install computers in his plant, computers that ran the machines, computers that regulated the computers that ran the machines. Jake said that pretty soon there wouldn't be anyone left to manage on his shift. He could always go back to maintenance, they hadn't found a computer able to do that kind of work yet, but he was worried about the younger men, those just starting out who were getting laid off. The majority of them were "good boys" but without any advanced education. He didn't know what they were going to do. Some had found other jobs, some had joined the military, most had just moved on.

Jake's company was also beginning to bring contractors in to finish installation and repair jobs that had previously been completed by employees. In his opinion, what the contractors did mainly was to add to the confusion. With all the coming and going, lines of communication and authority were breaking down. No one knew who was in charge of what anymore. He'd just about get a new man trained and the man would be transferred or replaced by a switch and a dial. Even though Jake had less people to keep track of, he said that his job as foreman was getting harder. Every time one of the men on his shift disappeared, the rest would grumble about him not taking care of his own, or selling out to management. They didn't understand that he had nothing to say about it. Or, more likely, they understood but were scared, and Jake was the only target they had to shoot at.

Jake said that he didn't enjoy working for the company as much as he used to. He said that the family atmosphere, the pride, and teamwork were disappearing. It was becoming more cut-throat. Just about everyone he knew, including himself, would be in serious financial trouble if they lost their job. Jake and Sharon were finally doing pretty well. They had a nice house, two cars, and a small motorboat to fish from down at the shore. One of their boys was entering State College in the fall. That made two out of their five children who would end up with a college education, and two of the others still had a shot at it. They were doing all right, but that was because both of them had been earning salaries since before they got married. Things hadn't been easy in the beginning. They'd needed to mind their pennies. At one point Jake had worked for four straight years without taking a day off for sickness or vacation.

Later on, when the financial part had finally begun to ease off, there'd still been problems. Most of these centered around the kids. It is hard to raise a family properly when both parents are away at work most of the day. While the children were young, Sharon's mother had stayed with them. Luckily, she lived close by. But when they had reached the junior high and high school age and had started feeling their oats, things had begun to happen.

One of the girls had gotten pregnant, probably on the living room couch after school. She wouldn't say who the father was, although they had a pretty good idea. She'd had an abortion, but the whole thing had been a disaster. It had torn the family apart. Eventually their daughter left home and took a job without finishing high school. Sharon couldn't help blaming herself. If she had been around more, she would have known something was going on. But there had been no choice, really. If they wanted to keep appearances up, to maintain respect, she had to work. And prices kept rising and rising, especially for the kids' things. A simple pair of pants or blouse wouldn't do anymore. Now everyone had to wear designer clothes. Most of the kids had part-time jobs and pitched in, but the way they went through shoes, for example, was hard to believe. Food, medical expenses—everything cost more and more.

Sharon just couldn't imagine what would happen if one or both of them lost their job. The house would be theirs, that was one thing. It was paid for. But all that work, all those years down the drain. Jake would draw some sort of pension, but nothing close to what he was bringing in now. And she hadn't been employed long enough to be eligible. The thing that worried her the most, however, was how Jake would deal with not working. He had been employed by someone ever since he was a kid. He said that he'd still have plenty to do, but he was a proud man and devoted to his company. He had said over and over that taking a job there had been the smartest thing he had ever done. In the old days he had known some of the top-level bosses personally. They had worked their way up, too, and appreciated the fact that without the support of the guys down below they were nothing. Today, however, most of the managers were college trained and sought as little contact with the hourly employees as possible. Jake said that a young engineer would appear on the floor and order an operator who had been running a machine 20 years to change a procedure, then would walk away without telling him why or without asking the man what he thought. In the old days that never would have happened.

Jake said that he didn't really feel part of the operation anymore. Since the company had been taken over by that big conglomerate, he and his crew had been treated more or less like pieces of machinery.

Jake didn't fancy being treated like a piece of machinery. No one did. Jake said that he sensed real problems coming. The economy and the country weren't working right anymore. Gears weren't locking the way they were supposed to. Eventually something was going to tear loose. He also sensed that none of the "experts" floating around acting like they had things under control understood the problems any better than he did. It was mainly bluff, a lot of words that didn't mean much. Jake said that someday it was all going to come home to roost, and that when it did, there was going to be trouble—real trouble.

2

UNMASKING THE CULPRIT

Individually and as a society we are in a state of flux. Individually we seem to be on the edge of something big, something very positive. However, we don't quite know how to get there, how to achieve it. As a result, we feel frustrated. Things are not what they ought to be; things are not what they could be; and why doesn't somebody *do* something to make the system work?

As a society we also seem to be edging toward something big. On this level, however, that something is frequently something we'd rather avoid because it smacks of confusion and danger. We want to change direction but seem stymied, blocked. Our rationalization for this situation usually begins, "I want to change, but it's the other guy, that guy over there. He's the one to blame! He's the one who won't let it happen!" Each one of us as an individual wants to help reorient society, but there's always a villain or a bunch of villains who stand in the way, who keep us from heading in a more positive direction.

At least in terms of society, then, we view man, or "the other guy," as the ultimate culprit. But is he really? Is the world really a "jungle," our instinct to pounce irresistible? Do we as human animals always, by definition, need to have enemies, need to be locked into bitter win–lose struggles? Are the aggressiveness and defensiveness that exert such a strong influence on our behavior attributable perhaps to genetic makeup?

I, for, one, think not. I refuse to place the bulk of the blame for our current frustrations and fears on the individual. We all, of course, during our struggle to survive and thrive, get angry at times. We also find warped people in every society, people who want very much to harm others. But I believe that the vast majority of human beings desire sincerely to be positive, to follow whatever form of the golden rule exists in their religion or code of ethics. The problem, in my opinion, is not so much one of evil, amoral individuals, as it is one of *a lack of appropriate balance.* A healthy self-interest is natural and necessary. According to Aristotle, it is the driving force behind human and societal development. I don't know of many who would disagree. But for a society to work, self-interest must be balanced with an appropriate level of concern for the whole. When that balance tips too strongly toward "self," and when the individual quest for fulfillment detracts from one's ability to make his or her required contribution, society suffers, and society is everyone.

It is also my opinion, however, that while the above is obviously part of the answer, it is too simplistic. There has to be more, much more, and the "more" has ultimately to do with definitions.

Over lunch one day I asked a group of managers to define the most important thing that corporations, as economic institutions, do. A half hour was spent talking about developing resources, improving the GNP, generating jobs, defining and satisfying markets, providing a quality product. My role was easy. I just kept asking, "Why? " Why do we want to develop resources, improve the GNP, generate jobs?" Eventually someone said, "I guess, then, that the most important thing that a corporation does is to meet needs."

"Whose needs?" I asked.

"The needs of customers, employees, suppliers, distributors, the people who live in the surrounding community."

"Which group is the most important?" I asked.

"Customers. Without customers we wouldn't exist."

"What about suppliers?" I countered. "Without suppliers you wouldn't have anything to sell even if you had customers. And without distributors you wouldn't be able to get it out even if you did have something to sell."

"I guess, then, that they're all important."

"No." I shook my head. "There is a most important group. It's the employees."

My declaration gave my lunch companions pause. They obviously liked it but at the same time weren't sure that they should. Eventually someone asked, "Why employees?"

"Because," I said, "if a company needs customers, suppliers, and distributors, employees go out and find them. But customers don't go out and find suppliers; suppliers don't go out and find distributors. The primary thing that companies must focus on if they want to excel is the satisfaction of employees' needs so that these people want to do their jobs."

Another pause. Finally someone said, "Well, maybe so. Maybe that's what it takes. I'm sure that at least the union officers would agree. But I know from experience that if this company spent its time trying to satisfy every employee's needs, we'd go bankrupt within a month."

Someone else said, "That's what communism tries to do, isn't it? Take care of everyone's needs? Are you advocating communism?"

"No." I shook my head again. "In the first place, in the long run, communism doesn't work. In the second place, I don't believe that communistic leaders and industrialists understand the nature of modern-day employee needs any better than we. They're stuck in the same rut."

This time the response came immediately and from more than one direction. "What do you mean by that?"

What, indeed, do I mean by that? How can I possibly equate the free enterprise and communist systems that are so diametrically opposed philosophically? Coming up with an answer to this question is not an easy task. One way of going about it, however, is to define what I think the needs of today's employee *truly* are, then to see if we, or anyone else, is satisfying them. With this course of action in mind, I would like to start off by speaking in the most general terms possible. My purpose here is to set the stage, to provide a framework for what comes later in the book. Gradually, then, I'll grow more specific.

In terms of organizing our work lives in particular but also our everyday lives, it is my opinion that people strive to fulfill two basic personal needs. The first is the need for continuity in terms of those things that make us secure. The second is the need for change. At first glance the two seem to be contradictory. Upon further reflection, however, we realize that they are not. Rather, they are the opposite sides of the same coin. They make up a whole.

The need for continuity involves developing a routine that we understand and with which we feel comfortable. It involves being able to pay the bills. It involves knowing what tasks we have to perform daily so that we can allocate our energies in the most resourceful way, knowing that dinner will be waiting when we come home tired from work in the evening, knowing that on Saturday mornings we can look forward to a play session with the kids. At work, it involves understanding our responsibilities, realizing that our boss blows up periodically but doesn't mean it, knowing that bets are taken on the weekend football games during Friday lunch. Security and continuity help reduce tension. They make life more comfortable.

When we talk about change, on the other hand, we are talking about stimulation. We are talking about making our lives more interesting and exciting, about learning how to deal with variety, about understanding and developing our potential as individuals. Change is an ingredient necessary to learning, to "being alive." It provides us with adventure, with challenge. In our quest for such adventure and challenge we often do a lot of unusual things. We return to school to study archeology. We take up a potentially dangerous sport like ocean racing or sky diving. We accept a job in Sumatra. Change gives our lives richness and fullness. It makes our existence more than just comfortable; it makes it interesting.

It should be obvious by now that the key to the relationship between these two sides of the coin is, again, *balance*—finding the right individual balance between continuity and change. It should be obvious also that this balance tips in different directions at different times during the normal life cycle. While we are in infancy, early childhood, and old age it tips toward continuity. Because so many things are new, change is an integral part of the early years. It doesn't have to be sought after. In old age, when physical and/or mental abilities begin to fade, most of us would rather eliminate as much change from our environment as possible.

It is during the "middle years," during our working years that the stimulation resulting from change is most avidly sought. People feel strong. We want to test ourselves, to probe for the outer limits of our potential. At the same time life has become repetitious. The newness has worn off childhood's discoveries. Personalities and tasks in the workplace have become monotonous. The routine begins getting us down. We have reached our prime but are not fully celebrating it. We want something exciting to happen, and after so many years of waiting at our desk, computer, or drill press, we are beginning to realize that if our adventure doesn't materialize soon, we will no longer be in a position to enjoy it.

A third obvious point is that without a degree of continuity firmly in place, change—no matter how stimulating—is not attractive. Continuity has to do with the basics, with being able to lead a decent life, with being able to provide for our families. When the requisite level has not been achieved by ourselves and those we feel responsible for, uncertainty and change are the enemy, a nerve-fraying trauma that people struggle to avoid.

In terms of discovering the appropriate balance between continuity and change, then, the workplace is obviously a critical arena. The majority of modern men and women spend approximately one-half of their awake lives between the ages of 22 and 65 at work. They spend roughly another quarter of their awake and often part of their asleep lives dealing with the aftereffects of work—trying to relax, getting reacquainted with their families, dealing with problems that have grown severe because they didn't have the time to address them initially.

From one point of view, work is an area where change is the enemy, where it is not well tolerated. Work is the wellspring from whence we gain the prerequisites to security and continuity. Work, therefore, should not be tampered with.

From another point of view, however, work is that area where change is most desperately craved. Due to the dull, repetitious nature of most jobs, employees have been known to generate all sorts of diversions, some quite creative, in order to keep mind and spirit alive. Watching the same computer screen all day, pecking automatically at the same typewriter, staring at the same figures, listening to the same dull, droning voice is difficult. Any variety is appreciated.

"But," we say, "there is change." The economic sector is in a constant and ever-accelerating state of transition. One doesn't have to read Alvin Toffler's *Future Shock* to see that. Technology is on a rampage. Businesses and entire industries are coming and going. The nature of our jobs is being altered on an almost daily basis. If anything, change is out of control. We're being swamped with it. We don't know what to do with it all. We don't know whether it's good or bad, whether or not it's avoidable, and we can't slow it down long enough to find out these things.

So here we are again, in an apparent contradiction. We read continually about the lack of stimulation and challenge in the workplace—not enough change. We also read continually about the ever accelerating rate of technological innovation and its impact on the workplace—too much change. Which is the correct impression?

I believe that both are. The problem is that we're not looking at the whole picture. There is a missing ingredient, a missing variable that we must add to the formula before we can understand it. That ingredient or variable is, simply, *control.* When we think about it, we realize that control is the key to our personal success or failure. First, as I have indicated, we feel a compelling need to establish control over the resources upon which our continuity is built. Until we do so, life's efforts will focus entirely on this task. Second, we also want to establish some degree of control over the amount of change in our lives. We want, ideally, to be able to regulate it like we do a water faucet, turning it on and off at will.

With this objective in mind, then, we can develop an answer to the question of how it is possible at the same time to have both too much and not enough change in the workplace. The "too much" is the variety that threatens our control in terms of continuity. The "too much" has to do with unexpected pay cuts or the loss of a promised raise. It has to do with having our financial benefits trimmed, with being relocated on short notice or against our wishes. It has to do with being "riffed."

The "not enough" concerns our lack of control over possible sources of desired change and excitement in our everyday lives once continuity is firmly in place. On the most mundane level, it concerns not being allowed to leave our desk. It concerns trying not to look at our watch too frequently and not to go to sleep during staff meetings. It concerns wanting to sneak out early on days when nothing is happening, or wanting to do a little shopping during lunch. It concerns being afraid to call a friend to break the monotony, or to carry on an office flirtation, or to make a paperclip chain instead of struggling endlessly on a report that has little meaning.

Historically, in terms of society as a whole, increased control over our environment and those inputs necessary to both continuity and change seem to have come in cycles. During "up" periods a well-defined order has emerged, advances have been made in the social as well as physical sciences, and the individual has gained a great deal of self-respect. In retrospect, however, every one of these "up" periods has eventually faded, losing its inspiration and enthusiasm. People have once again settled back into a dependency mode to wait for the next outburst of enthusiasm.

Why does this cycle occur? Do the people involved eventually tire of progressing and seek their "safe place" to rest for a while? I think not. Rather than willingly give up these progressive periods, I believe that the populations involved unwillingly lose their grip, helplessly watching such periods fade away. But how do they lose their grip? What is the cause? Who is the culprit?

My argument, as I have indicated earlier, is that the most basic culprit is frequently the *definitions* upon which we base our reality, and that because work life-related definitions have played a dominant role, if not *the* dominant role, in this reality thus far, they should be focused on.

But what work-related definitions, specifically, am I talking about? In order to ferret out these prime suspects, I suggest that we use the old "What?" "How?" "Why?" formula. Based on this approach we must first ask what kinds of work we actually do. Do we transform raw materials taken from nature or the lab into finished products? Do we gather, analyze, and distribute data or information? Do we provide health care for people? What different categories can this work be broken down into? Are we still involved in work detrimental to our well-being when we no longer need to be? What means do we use to accomplish organizational objectives, what type of management philosophy is involved, and, most important, how much *control* do we exercise over our activities? The "What?" question, therefore, obviously has to do with the core concept of *work* itself.

In terms of the "How?" question, we ask how modern-day employees are encouraged to accomplish their assigned tasks. Is money the only real incentive? If it is, what are its strengths and weaknesses in terms of our objectives? Is there something else to which we need to shift our focus? The "How?" question has to do with *reward systems.* How are these systems designed, and by whom? More important, what are they based on, and how have they evolved over time?

Concerning the "Why?" question, we ask why an organization exists, not in terms of the public this time, but in terms of its employees and their needs. We have pointed out that the ability of any organization to compete effectively in the marketplace and to adapt successfully to constantly changing demands rests ultimately on the existing level of employee commitment. The level of existing commitment, in turn, relates directly to the organization's ability to meet employee needs. When the organization fails to meet these needs, performance drops off. We must discover, therefore, what employees' true needs are and if our organizations are capable of fulfilling them. Do our organizations help satisfy the general need for continuity? What about the parallel need for change? Can they help satisfy the more specific needs that make continuity and change possible? The "Why?" question, then, has to do with the role organizations play in facilitating *overall employee development.*

To summarize briefly at this point, the "What?", "How?", and "Why?" questions relate to the kinds of work done and the way in which it gets done; the reward system offered to make employees productive; and, finally, the contributions that work does and should make to overall employee development. Work, rewards, and development, then, are three of the conceptual cornerstones of our work lives. It is my belief that many of the problems that we as a society are currently struggling with, that we as individuals frequently find so frustrating, must somehow involve one, two, or all three of these "cornerstones."

But what, indeed, are work, rewards, and development? One way to describe these three concepts is to say that they are the ways that we choose to accomplish objectives important to everyone. Leaders look at an area of life that has to be organized in order for society to function and progress, then define the best way to accomplish this organizational effort in terms of current knowledge and values. The key word in the last sentence is, of course, "define." Work, rewards, and development are, in fact, knowledge- and value-ladened definitions of how these three key aspects of our work lives should be organized.

This realization brings us to the main argument of my book. Our society's major problem, as I see it—the one underlying most of our confusion and frustration, the one we must deal with initially—is not bad management or self-centered employees. These are just symptoms. Rather, it is the fact that our current definitions of work, rewards, and development, the ones on which we are building modern-day organizations, the ones that shape our everyday work lives, are totally outdated. In fact, if we want to be more specific, they are, surprisingly enough, at least 400 years old! All three actually have their roots in the 16th century, in the Medieval period. As a result of this circumstance, we find ourselves in a very difficult situation. We are trying to map out an expanded 20th century universe using an obsolete 16th century telescope. What we see does not coincide with what we know to be possible. Our world, our abilities, our resources, and our values have changed greatly. Our definitions of work, rewards, and development, however, have not. Because they have not, the societies and organizations built on them are incapable of fully meeting the modern-day needs of their citizens and employees.

There are two more definitions that are important to the major task of this book, that of "redefining our work life reality." The first is the definition of the role of technology. The importance of technology to all our institutions has grown steadily, until today many consider it to be *the* critical consideration. We cannot, therefore, discuss work without discussing how technology must be redefined so that it will remain a positive force in both our individual and societal evolution. The second additional definition is one that will probably emerge as a natural result of our efforts to update the concepts of work, rewards, and development. It is a concept into which the other three feed. It is the concept of "success." What, exactly, constitutes individual success in today's world? How, ideally, *should* success be measured in a healthy society? Is the amount of money one earns, for example, the critical factor? Or perhaps this measurement should be based on the degree of knowledge achieved. What about our contributions to the welfare of others? Are they really important? How about the quality of life attained, or the amount of power one gathers? Can there, in fact, be more ways than one to succeed? Again, based on what we have been talking about, does success, as we currently define it, result in an adequate feeling of accomplishment? If not, why not? And finally, can modern man, in fact, be considered successful without really succeeding?

With the scenario presented in Chapter 1 and the questions posed in Chapter 2 in mind, therefore, the purpose of this book is twofold. The first objective is to redefine the key concepts of "work," "technology," "rewards," and "development" in the way that will help us to dig out of our rut, in the way that will allow us to achieve real success. This process will not be easy. Redefinition never is, and redefinition that affects fundamental beliefs can be bloody if not carefully thought out and presented. During these efforts I shall focus on the corporate world in particular. I shall do so because, in my opinion, this is still our most viable sector. The incentive remains strongest here to adjust, once the nature and direction of desirable change is understood. Another reason for my chosen emphasis is that once we have redefined these critical concepts, once we have realigned our priorities and begun moving forward again, I believe that the role of the free enterprise sector will shift and expand greatly. The sector will begin playing an increasingly important role in our achievement of both individual and societal success.

My second objective is to attempt to identify where these definitional changes can and should lead us. If you will, I plan to "idealize" the world of work, then to expand this idealization to other critical areas of our lives, showing what things are possible once we bring our work-related definitions up to date. But first, we must establish the foundation stones. We must redefine our reality before we rebuild it. We must begin by getting the concepts of work, technology, rewards, development, and success squared away.

Part II

THE STARTING POINT
FOR CHANGE

Societies create their own reality. They come up with their own definitions, then build their institutions around these definitions. The secret is that whenever they want, they can change the definitions, reconstruct their institutions and alter their reality. Don't let anyone tell you otherwise. All it takes, all that it has taken throughout history, is the realization that such change is possible, and the necessary degree of commitment.

3

THE TRUE NATURE OF WORK

Work is a word we all use freely. It has many different connotations. We might do a "good day's work." We have people in our organization who are "workaholics" and "workhorses." We "work a problem through." We "work out" on a dance floor or athletic field.

But what, actually, is "work?" In the traditional sense it is the way in which we expend our energies in order to achieve predefined objectives and to gain predefined rewards. Until relatively recently in modern history, up to approximately the Medieval period in Europe, all or most of such objectives and rewards had to do with survival. The majority of the population worked constantly—hunting, building, planting, migrating, fighting, crafting—in order to gain those things necessary for life. Eventually, however, due to the development of improved techniques for converting natural resources into finished products, survival became less of an issue. Instead, the rewards of work increasingly had to do with improving one's situation.

At this point, work became, for most, a large chunk of time and energy spent doing something that we do not particularly relish—reproducing the same table, basket, shirt, piece of cheese, gun, or service—over and over during our morning, afternoon, and sometimes evening hours so that our "leisure" or recreational time could be enjoyed and passed doing what we wished. This arrangement was formalized and given the ultimate stamp of approval by the 16th century Protestant Reformation. Martin Luther and John Calvin, the two priests who shaped the Reformation, defined industriousness as the key prerequisite to salvation. Their message was: Work hard, work willingly, no matter how odious your assigned duties may be. Without work, all is lost. They declared that the sacrifices made at work not only improved leisure time activities, but enhanced one's chance of gaining the ultimate reward, a trip to heaven.

Although gradually during the following centuries the religious connotation faded, the need to work and to sacrifice became ingrained in our cultural psyche as being critical to social acceptability. The unpleasantness, the drudgery of most jobs were simply crosses that had to be borne. They were a necessary part of the whole. This basically, then, is the rationalization with which we continue to struggle today. Although our situation and abilities have changed radically, although society has evolved and progressed in many respects, our definition of work has not. "Work" continues to mean being paid to expend energy in a company's or agency's interest so that we can play later. Even when there's nothing to do, we should find ways to expend energy. Clean your tools, reorganize your files. Call a staff meeting and make everyone give reports on what they are up to. Add another review step to the generation of a work order. Start a cost effectiveness project. Start a quality improvement project. Call in a consultant.

I would guess that a sizable chunk of all energy expended in our large, modern-day companies is expended on the above types of unnecessary tasks, or what I call "busy work." Busy work is that which, while giving an employee the appearance of doing something of value, contributes little to the bottom line. It helps the individual gain usually short-term rewards, but rarely facilitates the organization's achievement of its longer-term objectives. We all know co-workers who come in early and stay late, who always seem to be involved in some critical project, hurrying here, hurrying there, setting up meeting after meeting, but whose contribution is hard to define. At best, such pretense has no effect on overall organizational performance. At worst, it produces stress and two-way contempt.

Despite its questionableness in terms of benefits, many organizations still encourage such busy work. Most of us, I am sure, at some point in our careers, have had a boss who periodically toured his or her territory to make sure that everyone was "doing something and not just sitting around." Many of us, I am sure, have worked in an organization where it was understood that employees who wanted to progress upward through the ranks were expected to voluntarily give up part or all of their yearly vacation time because they were "just too busy." It is my opinion that few non-hourly jobs in either the modern private or public sector take more than 30 or 40 hours a week to complete adequately if the employee and his or her boss know what they are doing, plan properly, and coordinate their activities. Most take less, sometimes far less. Why, then, do we insist on putting in unnecessary time?

We insist, as I have said above, because we have been taught that work as we now know it is the only answer to our problems and to the satisfaction of our needs. This belief, however, can obviously lead to counter-productive as well as productive behavior. An example is the employee who doesn't know his or her job but believes that if he or she stays with it, puts in additional hours, something positive is bound to materialize. Work itself, because it is good, will provide a satisfactory solution. The willingness to sacrifice time, unfortunately, is all too frequently considered an acceptable substitute for the ability to get the job done effectively. To make matters worse, employers tend to give such people the benefit of the doubt because they are "keeping their noses to the grindstone," and "have the right attitude."

Another, all-too-familiar example of the counter-productive aspect of this belief is the person for whom work has become the essence of existence. Without it, such people eventually begin to believe that they have no identity. These are the individuals who talk compulsively about their jobs, who find excuses to return to the office during off hours because the office is the only place where they truly feel comfortable. These are also frequently the individuals we read about who die shortly after retiring.

The problem is that most of us still do not believe that an acceptable alternative to our traditional definition of work exists. It's not that our unimaginativeness has gone unchallenged. Over the years a growing number of thinking people have questioned this reticence to reevaluate. The most recent manifestation of such rebelliousness is the "quality of working life" movement that started voicing dissatisfaction approximately 15 years ago in earnest and has been receiving steadily increasing amounts of exposure. This movement, however, while having caught on intellectually, even in some instances emotionally, has not inspired an impressive number of concrete changes.

Most modern day upper-level managers can drop a whole string of the right buzz words—quality circles, participative management, autonomous work groups, self-determination, profit sharing. For them, however, as well as for the people under them, the time spent at the office or plant remains a repetitive, boring, tension-building drag. Our cultural conscience cannot accept the suggested modifications because they don't really have anything to do with work as we understand it in our gut. As a result of this mindset, while great and wondrous things beckon, we remain mired down in the mud of our 16th century mind-set. We are slogging along under a burden that should have been shed long ago. We are traveling cross country in an oxcart, our eyes glued to the ground, blind to the brightly colored possibilities whizzing past on the highway and in the air.

But how do we change? As I have said earlier, we must begin with the definition, the cornerstone. Only after this has been updated will we start to truly understand what is possible and be able to expel the ghosts of ages long past holding us back.

I recently read an article by J. K. Galbraith, "When Work Isn't Work," in the February 10, 1985, issue of *Parade* magazine that might give us a clue about how to start. Galbraith said, basically, that two types of work now exist in the modern industrial world. The first is the traditional type that we have been talking about. People spend seven to 10 hours a day, five days a week doing something they don't enjoy or profit from except in a monetary sense so that during off hours they can participate in activities they do enjoy. The second type of work is the kind that people actually enjoy or profit from other than monetarily. It is the type that allows them to learn, on a continuous basis, things that they consider to be of value. It is the type that offers a fair shake, the opportunity to advance or to change career directions if they desire. It is the type that encourages their contribution, that gives them a feeling of control over their situation. It is the type that provides a sense of continuity, progress, and even excitement.

Who does this second type of work? Galbraith mentions scientists, scholars, artists, politicians, and athletes. One proof of the difference, he says, is that while the average millhand or office worker looks forward with longing to retirement, scientists and scholars, although forced out of their positions at a certain age, frequently continue working of their own volition without pay. In this latter circumstance, the work itself is obviously a reward, as is the salary.

Both of Galbraith's types of work involve the expenditure of energy in order to achieve a predefined work-related objective and to gain desired rewards. The difference is in the way this energy is expended, as well as in the nature of the predefined objectives and desired rewards. Using these three criteria—energy expenditure, objectives, and rewards—I shall expand on Galbraith's start and venture to identify five types of work that encompass the modern-day whole. They are slave work, subsistence work, situation-improving work, developmental work, and leisure work.

In slave work, energy is expended to help achieve objectives defined by an owner rather than by the worker. The slave's only reward for this effort is survival. There have been, of course, various forms and degrees of slavery. Historically examples include cultures that have allowed slaves to earn their freedom. Scholars, artists, and public leaders rose from the rank of slave during the Hellenistic period in ancient Greece. The model used here, however, pictures the negative extreme of such work. In this situation individuals are forced by those more powerful to do work not of their choosing. The penalty for lack of cooperation is torture or death. Such slaves can be legally owned by their masters. Also, however, their condition can be forced on them by circumstances, the master not legally owning the slave but controlling all life-sustaining resources and opportunities within his or her reach.

Examples of this latter situation were plentiful during the early Industrial Revolution. Employees could not legally be held in slavery. However, due to lack of education, training, and resources, many could qualify for only the meanest factory jobs. Once hired, there was no escape. Salary levels were controlled entirely by employers, as were the availability and cost of food and shelter. Unions either did not exist or lacked power at this point. Employees spent their usually-short working lives trying unsuccessfully to get out of debt. They truly "owed their souls to the company store." The chances of putting funds aside so that they could improve their situation or move away were nil.

These workers gained neither continuity in terms of security nor the stimulation of positive change from their efforts. They had no chance to develop individual potential. They had no real learning opportunity, no chance to advance or change direction, no sense of control or progress, and a continual feeling of fear and dread rather than excitement. Slaves were dealt with more as pieces of machinery than as human beings. They were bought and sold or thrown out at will. So long as a reasonably low-cost supply of such "pieces" was readily available, the slave was expendable. Emphasis was on getting the maximum amount of work for minimum expense, with no consideration for the human dimension.

In the modern-day United States there are few remaining examples of slave work. It still survives in various forms in some small, isolated, agricultural towns. Also, there have been stories of migrant workers being pressed into slavery. But the trend is away from this kind of servitude.

The second category of work, subsistence-level work, centers on achieving "continuity" in terms of food, shelter, warmth, protection from enemies, and so on—and little else. People involved in it frequently live on the edge. When something goes wrong—a factory shuts down, a layoff occurs—they have to depend on the largess of the state or of others, or on crime to survive.

The major difference between slave- and subsistence-level work is that people doing the latter kind have a degree of choice in terms of how they expend their energy, what objectives they pursue, and what rewards they seek. The range of such choices, however, is limited. People in this group also have a chance to learn and to improve their situation. Hundreds of thousands of immigrants who began their lives in the United States as subsistence-level workers have done just that.

Subsistence-level work provides the possibility for a sense of accomplishment and self-identity. It allows for a certain amount of recognition, especially from those in the same situation. The fact that an individual is working hard and improving his or her status is generally respected. The opportunity for a quick turn-around, however, for rapid quality of life improvements, is small. Noticeable change usually takes a generation or more. Many never make it. Every major U.S. city contains pockets or even large neighborhoods of such people, laborers who, due to economic, social, physical, mental, or emotional constraints cannot gain the training, experience, or opportunity necessary. They have the freedom to change employers but lack the capability to improve their rewards, either in their current situation or by changing to a new situation.

A great many of our modern-day jobs remain in this category. Secretarial jobs, for example, frequently pay just enough to get by on. If the secretary has a spouse who works as well, their combined salaries can provide opportunity for improvement as well as survival. If, however, the employee is single, especially single with children, as are a growing number of today's women, then the situation is a bleak dead-end and is likely to remain so.

The third category of work, situation-improving work, includes most of the adults who read this book. They are the managers, the executives, the technicians, the skilled operators, the maintenance people. This category includes many of our typical nine-to-five jobs, the jobs that we do but don't really enjoy—so that our kids will receive the best possible education, so that we can afford a larger house or a summer place, so that we can drive a late-model car and eat out several times a week, so that we can tour the United States or Europe on vacation.

In situation-improving work we still have little to say about the way our energy is expended. The range of achievable rewards, however, is greatly expanded. Also, the work situation itself provides much greater opportunity than does subsistence-level work. It usually allows us to advance or change directions. Learning is involved, even required if one is to progress. The actual work done, however, is still usually dull and repetitious. The exciting moments are few and far between. More control is possible since if the situation gets bad enough people feel they can quit and find something else—but something else after the first few weeks that probably will not be much better. They will once again be a cog in some machine run by an insensitive hand.

The major differences between subsistence-level and situation-improvement work, then, are of degree rather than character. The amount of basic security achievable in situation-improvement work is much greater. The range of achievable rewards is also much greater. The degrees of learning and advancement possible, of excitement, of control have increased. But they have not increased enough to make the work enjoyable or to make people look forward to work as a positive part of their lives. Situation-improvement work is still sacrificial in nature. It is still something we'd rather not do. The pressures are less because we have backed away from the edge of total dependency in terms of survival. But they still exist. The rewards have improved, but they still do not satisfy many of our inner longings and needs. We enjoy a greater degree of continuity in terms of security, but the uncertainty, excitement, and challenge part of the equation is sorely lacking.

The fourth category is "developmental work." This is the second kind of work Galbraith described saying people actually enjoy or profit from it other than monetarily. Not only does it provide continuous security, but also change, stimulation, and excitement. It encourages creativity and challenges us. While involved in developmental work we have quite a bit to say about the way in which our energy is spent. We also have quite a bit to say about work-related objectives.

Developmental work is not new. Scientists, scholars, and artists, for example, have been around a long time. Early scientists and scholars, however, were few and far between. They usually came from the nobility or from extremely wealthy families. Artists were totally dependent on patrons for not only work, but for survival.

As technology matured and educational systems expanded and improved, the number of such jobs increased, first slowly, then, during the Industrial Revolution, explosively. Today, we have entire industries built around developmental work. Think tanks, research centers, and consulting groups, for example, spend their time expanding the limits of their own knowledge and abilities, as well as those of the client. The space and computer industries are built around such challenges.

Developmental work is not usually completed in a specific place during a specific period of time. Those involved are not as eager to walk away from it at five o'clock. It goes with them in their heads, their briefcases, their computers. It is a welcomed part of their lives. This is so because the work itself provides a sense of accomplishment. At least part of the reward gained is intrinsic. The salary earned frequently becomes secondary in importance.

Developmental work often can be done in the home or at least in an atmosphere far more relaxed than that found in the traditional office or factory. These more relaxed circumstances are further encouraged by the disappearance of the traditional "boss." The main role of the boss in slave, subsistence-level, and situation-improving work has been to assure that employees do their jobs, that they don't slack off, that they earn their pay. With developmental work, because employees *want* to do their jobs, the boss is transformed into a coordinator and facilitator. His main responsibility is to ensure integration of efforts and provide requested assistance.

The fifth kind of work, leisure work, is the kind we do when we're not at the office. It includes planting trees in our yard, working on our car, making curtains for the windows, up-grading our hi-fi set. It includes taking a course in astronomy when we are accountants, studying French because someday we might like to work in France, learning how to operate a computer, writing our memoirs. It includes volunteering to build a swing set on the local grade-school playground, or helping to clear a campground for the neighborhood scout troop.

Leisure work, in essence, is work that we do *when* we want to do it *the way* we want to do it *because* we want to do it. No one gives us orders. No one tells us to stop standing around. We are not paid for it. In fact, we sometimes pay for the privilege of participating. It does not, therefore, usually take care of the basics. It does, however, provide the opportunity for self-education, advancement, and change of direction, at least in one's own eyes.

Leisure work and developmental work obviously are closely related. In both, the individual exercises control over how his or her energy is expended. In both, the individual helps define objectives. In both, the reward is derived, at least partially, from the work itself. The difference is, again, one of degree. In developmental work one's expenditure of energy is not as thoroughly controlled by the individual. Project assignments are often based on expediency, cost considerations, or office politics rather than on the abilities and interests of employees. At the same time, while we can contribute to the definition of company and work objectives, our contributions might be ignored or altered in ways that we do not like. Because we are still dependent on such jobs for the provision of the basics, we have to accept these things. Not so with leisure work. Here we have almost total control over energy expenditure, objectives, and rewards. We can quit at any time without fear of unemployment. We can redefine our objectives from moment to moment without consulting anyone.

The key variable in all this, as stated in Chapter 2, is the degree of control exercised. In terms of our work life, then, in order to achieve an optimal degree of control, we should try to put together that combination of developmental and leisure work that maximizes the latter while, at the same time, allowing enough of the former to provide those goods and services necessary for survival and situation improvement. That is the ideal. That is what we are all aiming for.

As an exercise, let us now place slave, subsistence level, and situation-improving work in one category, developmental and leisure work in another, and compare the characteristics of the two. In terms of the first category, which we shall call "sacrificial," our work is done on command. Tasks are assigned and defined. Frequently an instruction manual exists, although no one can find it. Work in the sacrificial category is repetitious. We learn a task, a procedure, then repeat it over and over, with occasional slight modifications. Work in the sacrificial category is dull and uncreative. Even on the situation-improving level, while there is some learning, change, and challenge, the majority of our time is spent on tasks understood well enough to complete with one's eyes shut. Work in the sacrificial category supposedly fits into some master scheme. Usually, however, we have little or no idea of what that scheme is and are not sure that anyone else does. Work in the sacrificial category is controlled mainly by external forces. This control, however, is accepted so that one can achieve continuity in terms of security.

Work in the second category, which we shall call "new world," also provides security or is an outgrowth of preexisting security. Such work is frequently creative, at least in individual terms. It is fulfilling and challenging. It provides an opportunity for continual learning and self-improvement. Control rests entirely or mainly with the individual doing the work rather than with outside forces. Work in this second category is generally enjoyable and not constrained by time or space requirements.

What has our exercise shown? Well, it seems to me that we have just defined the difference between the way a machine operates and the way a human being is supposed to function. The machine is "told what to do." Its objective is designed or programmed into it. A machine is controlled totally by external forces. It is "taught" a task, then repeats it over and over with occasional slight modifications that it can be programmed to make. A machine cannot "create," at least not in the traditional sense. A machine and its operation have been designed to fit into a grand manufacturing scheme, of which the machine, of course, has no understanding. Finally, a machine is known to be functioning effectively when it is running, clanging, tweeting, grunting, and grinding out the widgets. Motion is the key indicator.

The human being, on the other hand, thinks, learns, creates, wants control over his or her life and activities, wants change, challenge, and excitement, wants to understand what's going on and how he or she fits. The human being functions most effectively when he or she has a say in how things are done, has a chance to help organize and improve the process. Motion is only one indicator, and a relatively unimportant one at that.

The obvious question at this point is, "If the alternative is, indeed, so attractive, why do we persist in our outdated mode of thought and action? Why don't we change?" Instead of continuing to substitute people for machines, why don't we allow machines to do as many sacrificial type jobs as possible and free people for the new world type work to which they are better suited?

"Sounds nice, but we can't do that." I hear.

"Why not?" I ask.

"It wouldn't work," I hear. "That's not the way our society is set up."

"Rubbish." I reply. "It's all a matter of definitions. The problem is with our definitions. Once we get these straightened out, we can do any damn thing we please."

In summary, then, our current definition of work is rooted in the 16th century. Way back then work was something to be endured so that one might enjoy his or her just desserts in the next life. During the Industrial Revolution we moved the target of all this sacrifice a bit closer and made it enjoyment of our leisure hours. We have discovered, however, that more than one type of work actually exists in today's world. There are, in fact, five different levels of work, based on the degree of all-important control exercised over how we expend our energy, on how our work objectives are defined, and on the range of rewards to which we have access.

On the lowest level is slave work. From there we climb through subsistence-level work, situation-improving work, and developmental work to leisure work. Most of us are stuck at the situation-improving level. We are still functioning as machine parts, doing sacrificial-type work, grinding it out, when one step away is freedom, the new world type work enjoyed by growing numbers. The question is, then, why can't we let the machines do what they do best and move on to the things that we do best? What's holding us back?

Part of the answer to this question is based on an understanding of the role that technology is currently playing and should play in industrial society. Our next topic of conversation, then, must be technology.

4

TECHNOLOGY:
FRIEND OR ENEMY?

Stan was laid off several weeks ago. He had worked as a staff manager
for a large electronics firm. The company was not doing well, although
it had a long, respectable history. The previous CEO had decided that
at least part of the problem was its failure to keep pace in terms of
technology, so he had started an investment program, buying and
installing state-of-the-art equipment, millions and millions of dollars
worth of it. The current CEO, however, worried by the continuing
drop in profits, by the related fall in the value of corporate stock,
and by the growing possibility of an unfriendly takeover, had re-
versed this trend, stopped the spending, and in an effort to improve
the corporation's financial image as rapidly as possible had instituted
cost-cutting measures, the first such measure being the elimination of
as many positions as possible.

The long-term objective of both these men, despite the difference
in their approaches, had been to improve the company's bottom line
by decreasing labor levels and, therefore, manufacturing costs. Technology was the key. In the first instance new technology was being
bought to *replace* workers. In the second, the technology already in
place was supposed to help take up the slack. This was nothing unusual, of course. This sort of thing happens every day. But the above
observation is critical to my argument. Keep it in mind and we'll get
back to it later.

When Stan learned that he had been laid off, he didn't know quite how to react. He'd lost jobs before—a bartending job during his carefree days, a research assistantship during his college career when a grant ran out. But he'd never lost a job at this level, at a corporate staff level. The severance package was extremely fair by current standards. He continued to receive full pay for one year, complete with benefits, excepting dental care and flight insurance. The corporation lined up a top-grade agency to help him find a new job. And besides, he had been traveling to the other end of the country almost weekly for the last several months to work on a project related to the new technology being installed and was worn to a frazzle. Getting laid off, therefore—especially in such a generous manner—was in some ways even a blessing.

Why, then, did Stan immediately find himself feeling depressed and even guilty? Why did he wake up on the dot of six A.M. Monday, Tuesday, and Wednesday mornings and rise to wander agitatedly about the house, even considering, at one point, driving by the office? Why did he tell some people he was on vacation? Why did he feel sheepish working in the yard on weekdays and avoid going into town until after five in the afternoon to mail the resumes that he was frantically shoveling out in every possible direction?

The answer to these questions, of course, is no secret. We all know why these things happened to Stan. That old devil, the Protestant work ethic, was performing its magic. He was busy proving that he was just as conditioned, just as hooked as the rest of us. He had been replaced, at least partially, by a machine or machines, and that hurt. Even though he hadn't really enjoyed his work, especially during the last year or so, it didn't seem fair. He felt as though he was no longer a full-fledged citizen of the modern world, and such status was unacceptable. The work had been draining. He had actually heaved a sigh of relief when the rumors proved true. His wife and he had some savings in the bank, though financial security wasn't really a concern because he had excellent credentials and experience and there were plenty of openings in his field. In the meantime, while he looked, he had more than enough to keep him busy around home. He could finish earning his MBA degree, he could get to know the wife and kids again, he could make those repairs on the garage that he had been putting off, he could even relax some and maybe go on a golfing vacation.

Despite all these "plusses," Stan continued to feel uneasy. He kept trying but couldn't entirely shake the pain, the guilt, the sense of being forsaken and disgraced. That was the truth of it, and once he had sorted his feeling out he had begun to suspect that his situation and reactions probably weren't unusual. More important, he had begun to realize that his getting laid off wasn't just a fluke. Instead, he had just witnessed first-hand what technology was doing to and was going to do to thousands and thousands of employees. He had been the victim of a very definite trend, one, he suspected, that would eventually precipitate grave social upheaval unless it was very carefully thought out and controlled.

With the above scenario in mind, then, the most critical issue for us to address in Chapter 4 is, obviously, just what types of problems might the above-examplified computerization of technology actually cause? Might it at some more advanced stage begin, in fact, to pose a serious threat to our economic and social stability?

The answer to these questions that swells immediately is a very loud and emphatic "Yes!" If we continue on our current path, stick to our current interpretation of the computer's potential and value, technology sure as hell could put us in a bad place, one we might have a very difficult time digging our way out of.

Before explaining this pronouncement in more detail, let us first look at this technological phenomenon that cost Stan his job in as positive a light as possible. We have come a long way. Historically, we have progressed rather rapidly from hand-made products to products manufactured by machines that were run by hand to products manufactured by machines that were regulated by other machines that were run by hand to products that are manufactured by machines that are regulated by other machines that are controlled by computers that can be manufactured and improved on by other computers.

That is a long way.

But now we have reached a critical juncture in our progression, possibly one of the most critical junctures in human history. In some ways *Work and Rewards* is a continuation of my first book, *Problem Solving For Managers*. It addresses a key question raised in Chapters 8 and 9 of the first book, which discuss the computer revolution and the effects it will have on the workplace in terms of job displacement. It was noted in the first book that, historically, technical innovations, while absorbing jobs in some sectors, have been the source of more jobs overall than they have made obsolete. The computer, true to form, has already spawned a great number and variety of new jobs. It is the opinion of many, however, that computers are different in a critical way from all previous new technologies and that this difference will eventually cause massive, permanent layoffs.

Let me elaborate on what I have said above because it is important. Historically, new technologies—the spinning jenny, the steam engine, the cotton gin, and so on—first displaced human muscle and delicacy of touch. Then they displaced certain parts of the nervous system in that electronic circuitry could transmit a relatively sophisticated series of signals to regulate complicated production processes. It was not until the advent of the computer, however, that technology gained the "intellectual" capability of logical deduction.

This capability allows the computer to make decisions, even "creative" decisions according to some definitions of creativity, and gives it the power not only to run the machinery of industry, but to manufacture it, maintain it, and improve on it as well. Computer technology, therefore, probably will eventually be able to do most of the new jobs it creates as efficiently as or more efficiently than workers could. As a result, it will not provide new tasks for employees to replace the ones it has made obsolete.

One way to avoid this scenario is to consciously use computer-based technology only to complement the worker, not to replace him. This alternative, however, is made unacceptable by our current interpretation of "free enterprise." Modern-day emphasis is placed almost entirely on efficiency, on finding ways to provide more for less. Labor in some countries, such as Taiwan, is cheaper than in the United States, which gives those countries an advantage. Three alternative approaches to this challenge are possible. First, labor costs in the United States can be forced downward. This has happened sporadically in a variety of industries. I do not, however, believe that such change can possibly represent a lasting trend so long as labor-management relations remain largely adversarial, so long as emphasis in the industrialized world remains on "growth," and so long as the threat of inflation exists. Pressure for salaries to climb is a natural result of these realities, and the worker has gained too much power to be denied.

Second, the price of labor can rise in countries where it is relatively low. This also is happening, but slowly. Industrial and governmental planners in these countries understand their advantage. They also realize that it is easier to inhibit the rise of salary levels than it is to bring them back down after they have climbed.

Third, we can invest in technology that produces more cheaply than human labor and use it to bring prices down and to improve our competitive status. It has been estimated that besides producing more efficiently, computer-based technology costs one-fourth to one-third as much as the average worker to install (train) and maintain (pay), at least in the United States.

When one country implements a computerization strategy in order to reduce costs and prices, others obviously will be forced to do the same. Currently, several countries with lower wage scales are actually leading the way. Japan, for example, is reported to have two or three times as many computerized robots in place as does the United States.

There is no doubt that the race is on. There is no doubt that members of the industrialized world community cannot afford to turn their backs on or underutilize computer technology if they are to remain economically viable. Daily we see estimates of the growing number of jobs technology is taking over and performing more efficiently. Many major corporations have already developed contingency plans for "total" takeovers.

But what about the worker? Are Karl Marx's worst fears about to be realized? Will the majority of our work force, indeed, be displaced by computers and end up spending most of its time waiting in line for welfare checks? Stan's ex-employer and many others are automating in order to cut costs and eventually increase profits. But whose profits? We are certainly not talking about an increase in the wages of the employees being put out of work. It's mainly the stockholders who are going to gain. As a result of this trend, then, a bunch of people will get richer and a larger bunch will get poorer, while those who still hold jobs will remain just about the same.

As this scene is repeated with increasing frequency across the country, our lower-middle and poverty-level classes will expand while our upper-middle and wealthy classes shrink. Obviously, we will also experience growing levels of unemployment. If the corporate world does not change, its response to this latter phenomenon will continue to be, "Not our problem. We're in business to make money. That's our role in the free enterprise system. We're not here to worry about the people we have to lay off."

The government, then, will have to take responsibility for these people. But the government will need increasing amounts of money to provide the necessary services. The amount it can draw through taxing individuals will no longer suffice. The middle class, which has traditionally provided the bulk of such funds, will be much smaller. In its need, the government will be forced to place an ever heavier tax burden on industry, and, *presto*, some form of instant socialism will spring up, with all its inherent inefficiencies and weaknesses.

No one will be happy. The unemployed will be unhappy because they have been forced onto the dole. Industrialists and stockholders will be unhappy because increasing amounts of their profits will be siphoned off. It will become rapidly obvious that if taxes keep rising companies will either have to leave the country, if there remains a suitable haven, or fight. As we all know, in order to survive, businesses must continue to make profits. Therefore, the business community, in self-defense, will be forced to unite and oppose further increases.

If any group comes out ahead in such a scenario, it will be the governmental bureaucracy. Government will have to expand rapidly in order to administer the new welfare state. Expanded government automatically brings increased regulation. Increased regulation kills incentive. Wealth and talent will start leaving the country. Because people will be sitting around waiting for their welfare checks, most of our population's potential will go to waste. Education for the majority will become pretty much of a farce. Entertainment will be the thing.

Because industry refuses to provide employment, the government will begin creating "busy work." It will fabricate jobs to let people at least pretend they still have some control over their lives. Crime will increase. The most popular passtime will rapidly become beating the system. Such sport will provide one of the few challenges left, one of the few arenas where people can still use their ingenuity. Those who succeed in beating the system, those who figure out ways to take advantage of it or ways to disrupt it will become folk heroes.

The government eventually will be forced to socialize industry due to its growing rebelliousness. But that will be okay because by this time all primary production and a major portion of the service sector will be fully automated. Even the bureaucrats will have trouble mismanaging such a setup. Anyway, by this time most of the work previously done by bureaucrats also will be handled by computers so that we will have regulatory computers interacting with production controlling computers—a very efficient system.

At the same time, however, life for the average Joe or Jessica gradually or not so gradually, will have become purposeless and uninteresting. Continuity of a sort will exist, but little or no uncertainty and excitement. The individual will have been crushed into a nameless data point stored in a mammoth data bank supporting our thoroughly automated socioeconomic system. Eventually, enough people will get fed up that we will have anarchy and rebellion and will be forced to start over, hopefully wiser.

Somehow, in this scenario we have slipped backward in terms of human development, rather than moving forward. Technology has pulled us out of one pit and dropped us into another. During the Dark Ages and early Industrial Revolution most people were trapped in poverty. Their struggle was to gain control of their lives and escape slave and subsistence-level circumstances. Technology played a key role, if not *the* key role, in helping them do so. Today, however, due to these same tremendous advances, we are headed for another trap, one nearly as lethal as poverty in terms of human development and loss of control. This is the trap of inescapable mediocrity.

And all this for the want of an up-to-date definition or two.

Technology, as we have said before, is currently viewed mainly as a *replacement* for workers. Its major role is to increase productivity and improve the bottom line by replacing workers. This was not always so. During the late 1800s and early 1900s in the United States, for example, technology had a different role. The economic situation then, of course, was not the same. For one thing, due to a rapidly expanding population and the newness of most products and processes, the market was almost unlimited. When Henry Ford decided that the best way to make money was to produce a car inexpensive enough for the masses to afford, things really opened up. While technology did eliminate some jobs, therefore, emphasis was on continual growth, so that the over-all labor force was continually expanding. As it expanded, more people had more money with which to buy things. As they bought more things, demand grew. Technology's role in this setting, therefore, was to help workers produce more and to buy more, and more of everything.

Eventually, however, we entered another era, one in which the market was no longer expanding so rapidly. New markets kept popping up, but production systems had grown so efficient that such markets became quickly saturated, frequently within a matter of years. Now manufacturers had to compete for customers. Emphasis shifted from increasing quantity to producing goods of acceptable quality more cheaply than the competition. Machines were better at this than laborers, so the latter started getting laid off.

That's where we are today. We have moved from an era where technology *complemented* employees to one where technology is *replacing* employees. As we have seen, however, this latest trend is leading us down a potentially dangerous pathway.

It is my belief, therefore, that the time has come to shift again and move into a third era. The shift I have in mind can be achieved by changing one word in our previous definition of technology's role. It is that simple. The word is *replacing.* Instead of replacing workers, the purpose of technology in this new era and definition should be to *free* them.

Groans, I hear. "Sure, fine," I hear. "Here it comes, romantic, pie-in-the-sky jibberish."

Maybe, but once we relate this modification to our new, five-level definition of work the "jibberish" might begin to make sense. Think about it. First, the market for developmental work is infinite. It will expand just as rapidly as we want it to and never become saturated. As a result of this phenomenon we will be able to utilize technology to the fullest possible extent without replacing workers. Also, because this market is infinite there will be no limit to the number of people who can find jobs or help create jobs in it for themselves.

This might be the more important observation that I make in this entire book, so I'd better elaborate on it.

We have, thus far, defined several progressions in terms of work. We have progressed from slave and subsistence-level to situation-improving to developmental work. We have progressed from work in which we had little or no control over how our energy is expended, over who defines our work objectives, over who defines the nature of our rewards, to work in which we have some.

There is, however, a third, critical progression that is important to my argument. We have also moved from an emphasis on the production of material goods or "pieces," to an emphasis on the provision of services and are now progressing toward an emphasis on the generation of information and ideas. Developmental work has mainly to do with the generation of information and ideas. This shift, in itself, erases almost all our previous limitations in terms of employment.

By way of explanation, the number of jobs available in the primary production sector traditionally has been limited ultimately by the number of product pieces that the market will absorb. The number of tasks that production levels will support has then been divided between workers and machines. When we talk about the service sector the same is true. The market is limited. The number of positions is, therefore, also limited, and computers are taking over a growing percentage of these.

When emphasis shifts to the generation of information and ideas, however, this constraint disappears. The market for information and ideas is constantly expanding. No known limits exist. Because the market is constantly expanding, no trade-off between human and computer hours is necessary. Technology again *complements* rather than *replaces* workers, both now doing what they are best suited for. In developmental work, employees focus on defining desired ends, objectives, and the best way to achieve these when cultural, emotional, and technical considerations are all taken into account. Workers and computers jointly think out the best implementation strategy. Computers take over when we get to the actual production process.

The same is true for leisure work, with one added guarantee. Because the participant, by definition, has full control, technology will play whatever role is desired. Leisure work's personalized and self-centered nature prohibits a takeover. At the other extreme, slave work has hopefully been eliminated, although instances of it keep popping up in unexpected places. That leaves subsistence level and situation-improving type work. These are the areas in which technology is having the greatest impact in terms of job loss.

What we are talking about, then, in essence, is *freeing* people from subsistence level and situation-improving work so that they can move on to developmental and leisure work.

Such a perspective raises a whole different set of questions. Previously the questions were: "How can we support those put out of work by technology without sapping our economic strength?" "How can we keep them out of trouble?" "How do we keep them busy or distracted?" "At what point should we start limiting the use of technology?" Now, we begin asking things like, "How fully can we automate subsistence and situation-improving types of work?" "How can we overcome existing technological limitations?" "What resources are required to encourage and facilitate the best balance of developmental and leisure work for a major part of the working population?" "How should we reorganize our management and societal systems in order to facilitate this change?"

This latter is obviously a more positive challenge. Instead of laying people off and wasting their potential, we would be involving a good percentage of the labor force in work better suited to their talents, work for which they are better equipped. In this new role they would be making a more valuable contribution than when functioning simply as machine parts. A second advantage of this perspective is that instead of distributing tax money in the form of welfare and gaining very little in return, we would be investing it in positive change, in reorganizing our institutions in a manner calculated to produce results beneficial to society.

Not everyone freed from subsistence level and situation-improving work, of course, would be capable of designing a perpetual motion machine or of discovering a cure for cancer. During my 15 years as a management consultant, however, most of which have been spent on factory floors or in support staff offices, I have been continually surprised by the results workers produced when presented with a challenge and when supported in their efforts to meet it. The problem, it turns out, is not so much their lack of intelligence or understanding. Rather, it is that no one has previously bothered to include them in design, planning, or problem-solving efforts.

Obviously, work as we now know it would pretty much disappear in such a scenario. Some of us would continue going to an office or shop, but most would be through with time clocks, morning review, going through the proper channels, and dressing the right way. I saw a television advertisement a while ago that seemed pretty much on target. The scene opened with a man in a sweatsuit cycling through empty streets in the early morning, his dog trotting alongside. The man arrived at a small office with maybe three or four other desks in it. No one else was there. He sat down and began working at a computer terminal. The next scene showed him talking on a telephone. He said, "I'm just about through, honey. I'll be home in time for breakfast." According to my fantasy, he meant, "I'll be finished with my day's work by then."

But wait a minute. Even if such a lifestyle were possible, would people want it? Do we really desire that much control, that much open time? Would we be able to cope with it? Or would it threaten us, make us hostile, or perhaps even slothful?

In my search for answers to the above I ran a very informal survey. I asked everyone and anyone I dared the following question: If things changed and you had to spend, say, only one-half the time you do now at work in order to earn enough to live comfortably; if, at the same time, you became pretty much your own boss and spent most of your working time addressing problems and making improvements rather than following orders or procedures, how would you feel? Would you miss the old way?

Responses fell generally into five categories. The first started out, "It will never happen, so there's no use in talking about it."

"Why not? Can't you imagine a world in which this situation existed?"

"The government, those in control wouldn't allow it. Most people have to be told what to do with their time. Give them too much freedom and they get into trouble. We'd probably have more alcoholism and drug addiction. People would perch in front of their television sets, or wander around looking for ways to relieve their boredom."

"What about the second part, about being more your own boss?"

"I told you, people have to be told what to do or they just get into trouble. It would be a disaster."

The second type of response, which usually came from upper-level managers, began, "Yes, I'd miss it. I enjoy what I'm doing now. Why would I want to give it up?"

"You mean there aren't other activities in your life that you enjoy as much as or more than your job?"

"Sure, there are plenty of other things I enjoy. But work provides a focus for my life. It has a lot to do with making me who I am. When I'm on the job I can make things happen. It gives me such a sense of accomplishment that I don't mind putting in extra hours. Another thing. Work makes leisure time activities more enjoyable. If I could do anything I wanted anytime I wanted to, I'm not sure I would enjoy it as much."

"What about the second part, about being your own boss?"

"I'm already my own boss. Harry leaves me alone as long as I produce."

The third type of response to my question fell into what I labeled the "noncommital shrug" category.

"I don't know."

"What's the problem?"

"I'd have to think about it. Most of my friends are at work. I don't have many outside interests."

"Could you develop them?"

"Probably, but I'm not sure."

"You don't think there'd be enough to do? You don't think you'd keep your old friends, or make new ones on the outside?"

"It's not that. It's just that I've never not worked. It would seem strange to me. I wouldn't be comfortable."

"Why not?"

"I don't know. I just don't think I'd feel right."

"What about being more your own boss, having more control over what you do? Would you like that?"

"I don't know. I've never worked without a boss."

The fourth category of response and by far the largest, far larger than all the rest put together, started out with some form of "Hell, no, I wouldn't miss what I'm doing now. I'd give it up in a minute."

"How would you spend your time?"

"I'd like to do more things with my family. The kids are growing up too fast. I'm missing too much. We'd like to travel, if we had the money."

"You'd have the money."

"I'd like to buy and rebuild a Model-T Ford that I've been eyeing. I used to work on cars when I was younger."

"Honestly, don't you think you'd eventually miss what you're doing now?"

"Maybe a little at first. But I'd get over it."

"What about your friends at work? Wouldn't you miss them?"

"Would I be the only one out of work?"

"No. Everyone would be in the same situation."

"Then I'd keep them. We'd find other things to do together."

"What about the stories concerning people who find they have nothing to live for once they retire?"

"That's not me. I'm taking a carpentry class now. We have a little place up in the mountains. I'd like to work on it. I'd probably also get a small house trailer. That way we could travel cheaper and stay for a while in the places we liked."

"What about the second part of the question, being more your own boss and focusing on problem solving and improvements?"

"It would sure beat the hell out of the way things are set up now."

The final type of response began with a puzzled silence. "Well, I guess I could use more free time, but I'm not sure."

"What do you mean?"

"When I'm working on a project I usually put in whatever time I think necessary. The number of hours isn't really a consideration. I don't usually worry about free time."

"What about your family? Don't you want to spend more time with them?"

"I frequently work at home. I mix my family life with my work life."

"What about the second part of the question, the part about being more your own boss and working on problems and improvements?"

Another silence. "I'm not exaclty sure of what you mean. Our team meets once a week to discuss project progress and problems. Ed's actually our boss, but he functions more like a team member most of the time."

At the end of my survey, when I added everything up, it seemed that the "ayes" definitely have it. Most people would quite willingly do away with work as we now know it. More and more people are realizing that it is, more than anything else, a very bad habit, a compulsive habit, like eating too much, the roots of which are buried so deeply in the past, in our social psyche, that we have been taking it as a given.

But it is not a given, not at all, especially now. Gradually, we are beginning to understand that we can transform work into something much more positive in terms of our personal lives. The necessary actors are all on stage. We have those already involved in developmental work to provide an example of what could be. We have the growing general realization that something is out of whack, that with all this affluence life should be better. We have the technology necessary to take over almost all primary production jobs and a rapidly growing percentage of jobs in the service sector.

What, then is missing?

"Yes," I hear. "If this is such a good idea, if the situation is so ripe for change, if all the necessary actors are on stage, why aren't we moving more rapidly? Why is there so much resistance if the benefits are so obvious?"

One reason for the slowness of movement cited above, which bubbles immediately to the surface, has to do with the lack of necessary comprehension. Technology is still the enemy in terms of employment and, therefore, is to be resisted. People who say that technology is doing a favor by taking away jobs are trying to set us up. Time and an appropriate, massive educational effort, complete with live examples of the benefits gained, will be required to convince and to gradually overcome this obstacle.

That's the easy part. Now we get into the hard stuff, the second obstacle. This obstacle will be much more difficult to deal with because it is so much more deep-seated in terms of both individual needs and our social history. This second obstacle has to do with the way we currently go about accomplishing our work. It involves the difference between *what we say* goes on in the workplace and *what actually happens.* It centers on two major roadblocks hampering our transition to "new world" work. The first is the conflict atmosphere found in most work environments. The second is the enduring reign of the "politicians." In Chapter 5 we will address both of these issues, then, and their deleterious effects on our efforts to improve our situation.

5

LIFE IN THE TRENCHES

In Chapter 3 I talked about the nature of work in general and how it is, or ought to be, evolving. In this chapter I want to become more specific and discuss how we actually go about doing what it is that we do on our jobs, and how it interferes with our efforts to progress.

One common characteristic of at least the first four types of work discussed—slave, subsistence-level, situation-improving, and developmental—is that those in charge are currently encouraging, or at least are pretending to encourage, a "team" effort. In our organizations we find shift teams, operating teams, project teams, problem-solving teams, and management teams. This attitude and emphasis results at least partially from our childhood conditioning. We grow up in a society that stresses team sports and teamwork above almost all else. Football, baseball, and basketball are the big three, and soccer, ice hockey, field hockey, lacrosse, and volleyball are others. In grade school, high school, and college most of us participate in at least one of these sports, either formally or informally, on school teams during recess, or on a vacant lot or city playground after hours. Even the individual sports like tennis, swimming, track, wrestling, and gymnastics that we enjoy stress team spirit.

As we grow older and spend less time playing an active role in sports, we begin supporting our local amateur and professional teams. We learn very quickly while sitting in the bleachers or in front of our television sets that no matter how great individual skills are at this level, if players don't complement and encourage each other's strengths, the team isn't going to win. The whole has to be more than the sum of its parts. Hotdog teams rarely cut the mustard in the big leagues.

It is obvious that, with this background, the team model, one that fosters a thorough, mutual understanding of everyone's role, one that stresses the best integration of skills, is a natural for our world of work. Such a transition makes good sense as we see with developmental-type work, where it is generally a given. To our continuing surprise and consternation, however, a successful transfer of this approach to subsistence-level and situation-improving situations rarely seems to occur, on a large-scale basis at least.

The problem that we must address is that so long as this transformation does not occur, the desired shift toward new world type work will be impeded. Too many of the characteristics critical to the new world model are possible only in a team atmosphere where conflict is held to a minimum, and when that atmosphere does not exist, the desired characteristics cannot emerge. It is not that continual attempts aren't being made to turn employees in sacrificial type jobs into teammates who complement each other in ways that allow the company to win. The advantages of such an arrangement are obvious. For one thing, teams have a better chance of coming up with the right answer. For another, a team is more likely to get a new idea implemented than is an individual. For a third, the team approach allows members to take greater risks in that they are not facing the storm alone. Also, a team effort provides more opportunity for stimulation as ideas clash and syntheses occur. Finally, a well-integrated team is generally capable of gaining much greater control over its situation than an individual and of moving more quickly and smoothly into the realm of new world work.

We all understand these things, yet our efforts continue to fall short. They fall short for several reasons. The most basic is that sacrificial type work excludes, almost by definition, the possibility of a true team effort. For one thing, team members have to be able to think and react. Employees functioning as machines aren't trained to do so. Also, team members do best when emotionally involved. Employees used as machines are not supposed to get involved. Their charge, clearly and simply, is to follow standard operation procedures. The less emotion displayed, the better.

Another reason for this failure is the constant conflict that modern day employees have to deal with, especially in sacrificial work situations. I am not talking about competition, I am talking about conflict, and it is not between corporations but between the individuals within a corporation. Competition has always been an inherent part of the team-building process. It is healthy. It makes us try harder, helps to develop our potential, and gives us confidence. We compete for attention with our ideas and actions, we compete for positions. But when the coach announces the plan of attack and the starting line-up, we put all that aside and cheer our fellow players on, encouraging them to do their best even if we are sitting on the bench. We are part of a team. We win as a team or lose as a team.

Conflict is something else. If we moved what goes on in today's major corporations out onto the playing field, we might have the following scenario. The Walbash football team has the ball and is driving down the field. The left guard, however, is upset that the left tackle has just made three good blocks and has excited the fans. During the next huddle, therefore, while the tackle is not looking, the left guard ties his shoe laces together so that on the next play he falls on his face and misses his block, drawing boos. Meanwhile, the left guard tries to cover both assignments, make two blocks, and draws cheers. But he can't do it alone, and the running back gets creamed for a 15-yard loss. During the next huddle the left tackle looks around, sees the left guard smirking, and realizes who the culprit is. However, there's no one to whom to complain. The coach hasn't bothered to show up, and the rest of the players are too busy arguing over what the next play should be, who should carry the ball. Instead of blocking the next time up, therefore, the left tackle turns and breaks the left guard's jaw with his fist, and the runner gets creamed for another 15-yard loss.

Conflict results from our desire and, sometimes, our need to beat the other guy. I recently dined with an extremely successful young executive from a large brokerage firm. During the meal we talked about his career and his rapid rise to a vice presidency. At one point I asked him what he had found most rewarding thus far. Was it the money he had made, the respect he had earned, the power he had gained, the prestige? Without hesitating, the fellow replied, "No, the most rewarding part has been beating people." He nodded. "Nothing else seems as important. Nothing else makes me feel as alive."

"By 'people' you mean competitors from other brokerage firms?"

"Not necessarily."

"Customers?"

"Not necessarily."

His response startled me, though I wasn't sure why. He seemed to have quite a few friends at the office; he was usually at the center of things, laughing, telling jokes, controlling the tempo. "You're not talking about the people with whom you work?" I asked. "You aren't including them in this, are you?"

"Yes, I do include them. If any of them got a chance to make me look bad, they wouldn't hesitate a minute."

"You don't really believe that, do you?"

He smiled. "I know it for a fact. It's happened."

"What about your friends outside of work? How do you keep these feelings from spilling over?"

This time he didn't smile. He hesitated, then said quietly, "Sometimes I don't."

While the conflict mentality is increasingly nonproductive concerning our development as both individuals and a society, its origins are, again, quite understandable. Survival is our most basic instinct. When shortages of those things necessary to survival exist we will do anything to gain them. We will steal. We will fight. We will kill. We will intimidate. No rules are respected. We will do what we must.

Once we have progressed beyond survival issues, however, it is usually to our advantage to start easing off so that we can concentrate on other objectives. This has happened to a degree in our society, but, in the final analysis, we are still fighting it out. We continue to react to arguments developed approximately 100 years ago by men like Herbert Spencer and William Graham Sumner, arguments that are no more appropriate now than they were then. These arguments, drawing loosely on Darwin's theory of evolution, say that, like nature, human society and the business world in particular should be governed by a "survival of the fittest" mentality. Citizens and employees should put their own self-interest first and fight anyone who gets in the way. The argument says that this "law of the jungle" approach provides the best means of allowing the most talented people to achieve the greatest degree of success and, as a result, to benefit society.

For the person capable of thinking about nothing but his or her own immediate gain, this is a very convenient rationalization. For the growing number of people, however, who care more about the long term, about the survival and success of the corporation or society of which they are a part, it is, at best, inadequate. For one thing, Spencer and Sumner failed to take into account a critical difference between the rest of nature's beasts and ourselves, which is that no other "jungle fighter" is capable of improving on, of continually making more effective his tools and techniques of conflict and destruction.

But why, if we understand the value of cooperation and competition and the deleterious effects of conflict on our attempts to move on to new world work, do society's efforts to encourage the former so frequently degenerate and end up producing the latter?

Part of the reason, I believe, is that two ingredients critical to healthy competition between teammates are missing in the corporate world. The first is a set of universally agreed upon rules of sportsmanship. No such animal exists. There are plenty of rules when we talk about how companies can interact with each other, but within individual firms there are very few controlling the way employees treat and use their teammates. At best we have a gentleman's agreement. Such agreements, however, usually fall by the wayside when times get rough.

Second, even if such a set of rules did exist, we usually lack someone with enough clout to enforce them. Everyone in the corporate world is a player, everyone is involved in manipulating circumstances for personal gain. No one person or body of people exists that is impartial enough to have the unquestioned authority to call "foul," to take players out and punish them when they do things to each other not in the best interest of the firm. What I am talking about, obviously, is a coach. All teams have a coach, either formally or informally. A team does not exist without a coach; coach is part of the definition. The coach's responsibilities include spotting and collecting talent, putting together the best combination of players, encouraging them, making sure they do their jobs and support each other, dealing with prima donnas, and keeping the team charged up but under control.

In a corporation trying to foster the team spirit we might assume that the president would take on the role of coach. Frequently, however, the necessary transition from player to coach has not occurred at this level. In order to function successfully in the latter role, a president must be able to rise above peer infighting and assume a degree of impartiality. He must be able to gain the respect and trust of his players as a leader who knows what he is doing. Many presidents seem incapable of doing this. But why?

One way to begin addressing this question is by defining the kinds of skills that are most critical to successfully running any organization. Noel Tichy, in his book *Managing Strategic Change*, identifies three traditional ways of viewing organizations: from a technical, cultural, and political perspective. He then talks about organizations that have technical, political, and cultural orientations. In order to serve the purposes of *Work and Rewards*, I have reworked his categories, which I believe to be all-encompassing, and used them to identify the types of skills possessed and practiced by employees on all levels. I have also given these three categories positive and negative connotations, which Noel does not do.

According to my at least partially-new interpretation, then, *technical* skills have to do with an employee's grasp of the tools and techniques necessary for adequate or superior performance. What are his or her financial, marketing, accounting, production, and human resources skills? How efficiently does the individual carry out his or her part of the process? How open is he or she to innovation, to new ideas, to finding out about other tools and techniques important to the operation, and about how his or hers complement them? Cooperation is obviously necessary to the enhancement of individual technical skills.

Cultural skills have to do with an employee's understanding of the management side of the operation and of how it fits with the technical side. It has to do with an understanding of how the organization as a whole functions, of what the key systems such as communications, problem solving, and work design look like, of why they are effective or not. It has to do with understanding how to interact most effectively with others in order to achieve corporate objectives on both an individual and a team basis. When one is improving cultural skills, emphasis must be on cooperation.

Political skills, according to my new, value-ladened interpretation, are those that enable an employee to manipulate others in ways necessary to advance his or her own career. Emphasis here is on competition in the best possible scenario and conflict in the worst. Rather than sharing critical technical expertise and cultural information, employees practicing political skills try to learn as much as they can from others while offering as little as possible in return. The goal is to use one's own power or that of others to "beat" peers, to make oneself look good and others look bad.

In new world organizations, technical and cultural skills are considered the most important. Emphasis is on developing and enhancing these. In sacrificial work type organizations the emphasis too frequently is instead on sharpening political skills. It is on learning how to build and defend isolated empires rather than on broadening one's horizons. The employee who can hold his or her liquor and is willing to spend the necessary hours socializing with or listening to the problems of superiors and peers is frequently more likely to progress than the technically-skilled performer who goes home right after work. Cultural skills also take a back seat because attention is too often focused on individual conflicts. Combatants are more interested in "one-uping" than in learning something of value from each other. They are too focused on short-term skirmishes to pay much attention to the big picture.

Despite the obvious frustration generated by such an atmosphere, many corporations actually encourage it. An example of this mindset was recently offered by one of our nation's largest banking firms. When its CEO retired, the board of directors governing this firm posted the names of three high-level officers being considered for his position, then proceeded to sit back and watch them fight it out.

One of the immediate results of this strategy was a rapid decline in overall corporate staff moral. The people that I know who were in relatively high-level positions at the time could talk about little else. Everyone was nervous about their own situation, trying to decide with which of the three to cast their lot, or how best to balance their attentions so that each of the three felt supported. Suspicion and mistrust developed. People were frequently afraid to talk to each other for fear of being misquoted. Vital communications got misrouted, the tension level climbed steadily, and rumor became the order of the day. When the decision finally did come down, one of the two losers was soon neutralized by the winner, who shifted him to a post where he no longer had real influence.

It's hard to believe that any group of mature, reasoning human beings could consider such an approach beneficial to the organization as a whole. Yet, we all know that this sort of exercise and waste occurs almost daily in the corporate world. Its stated purpose, as Spenser and Sumner have said, is to allow the cream to rise to the top. If by "cream" we mean those most politically oriented, those best versed in the wiles and ways of conflict, we might be right. If, however, by "cream" we mean the most technically and culturally skilled, we are frequently wrong, too frequently to take the chance.

It is fairly easy to spot presidents and other bosses who depend mainly on their political skills for advancement. For one thing, they are usually paranoid. The enemies they have made on the way up, of course, help to generate this paranoia. Its main cause, however, is the deep-down realization underlying their bravado that they don't really possess the technical and cultural understanding necessary to run the operation effectively. As a result of this insight they are wary of people with the skills they lack. They surround themselves, instead, with other politicians who "talk the same language," and with whom they can form the necessary alliances. The role of these confederates is to tell the president or boss what he or she wants to hear and to support his or her ego. They help create a customized reality that serves his or her self-defined purposes.

Therefore, while the president or coach with technical and cultural skills strives to open communication channels to as many of his players as possible and constantly expands his network in order to keep his overview up to date, the president whose rise to power has been based mainly on political skills tends to isolate himself as a protective measure. He includes fewer and fewer employees in decision-making exercises because he doesn't trust their motives or their understanding of his customized reality. At the same time, a political president feels a strong, continuing need to impress underlings with the fact that *he or she is, indeed, in control.* This need precipitates periodic appearances in the "trenches" to announce policy changes based largely on the president's own intuition. Such pronouncements are usually made with much fanfare and rarely produce the desired results.

Putting all the above together, it becomes fairly obvious why political presidents have trouble being accepted as coaches. It also becomes increasingly clear that the atmosphere in "political" organizations is not really conducive to the desired progress toward new world work. I don't believe that many employees enjoy working for companies where the politicians hold sway, where conflict is the dominant mode of interaction. It would be my guess that most prefer, instead, an environment where cooperation, or at least well coached competition, is the norm. But who is going to begin the shift? Who is going to take the chance? Who is going to say, "Okay, I'm tired of living with this constant tension. From now on I plan to do everything that I can to help my fellow employees. Hopefully, when the rest of you see that I mean it, you'll reciprocate."

"Sounds good." I hear. "But let the other guy start things off. If I tried something like that, first, the people I work with would think that I've flipped out. Second, Peter Jones would be on me in a minute. He's been waiting for an opening like this. He knows that I understand the job we do better than he ever will. He's out to get me, and this would be his chance."

Another thing that impedes the desired transition is that the politicians, who survive and thrive on competition, have a bad habit of winning when pitted against advocates of cooperation or competition. Let me offer the following scenario to further illustrate this point. In the operations department of the Wazon Corporation there are three people working on the same project who are after the same promotion. Their boss's decision as to which one gets it will be based on their compared contributions. They know each other, and one day they discuss the situation.

The first, Grace, is cooperation-oriented. "Look, if we work together, help each other, share information, we'll put together a successful project and all come out ahead. Only one of us will end up with this promotion, but the other two will also look good and will be at the head of the line when something else materializes."

The second, Luke, who is competition-oriented, shakes his head. "No, Grace, I can't do that. It sounds nice, but I wouldn't feel right. You have to go for it when you get the chance. I want that promotion. But I'll agree to this much. We won't help each other, but I won't try to make you look bad either. That way we can remain friends."

Ralph, who is conflict-oriented, listens carefully to both. Then he smiles warmly and nods in agreement. "Whatever you say. Grace, I'll share whatever information I have, and, Luke, we won't try to make each other look bad. The most important thing is that we remain friends. In fact, I'll begin stopping by your offices periodically to see how I can help."

The chances are that Ralph will win the position. Because he is conflict-oriented and sees everything from a "win-lose" perspective, he will say whatever is necessary to gain the confidence of his adversaries. He will, at the same time, work to widen the gap between

Grace and Luke so that he is the only one receiving information from both. Finally, when it is to his advantage, he will not hesitate to use this information to make his peers look as bad as possible. Ralph, due to his political perspective, will, in effect, agree to any rules of the game that the others suggest, but then, when convenient, will ignore them.

In summary then, if we want to progress toward new world work and an effective team approach, we must do two things. First, we must move beyond conflict as our principle framework for employee and unit interaction. In a conflict atmosphere, so much negative energy is expended on keeping others from getting ahead or on keeping them from getting even that very little or no progress is made. Second, we must discourage the politicization of management. Those whose skills are mainly political encourage conflict among subordinates as a means to maintain control. At the same time, they see attempts at cultural change as threatening, as an assault on their carefully constructed defenses.

In developmental work, neither of the above factors seem to play as important a role. But why don't they? What makes the difference? In order to answer these questions, we must identify the root producers of conflict and political dominance in our sacrificial work environment. We might just be talking about more bad habits. But, then, even bad habits originally have some cause. Let us now try to isolate that cause.

One agreed-upon observation about conflict is that it always involves a struggle over a prize of some sort and that the involved struggle basically is what pits us against each other. This observation brings us to our third foundational definition, that of "rewards," and specifically in this case, of corporate rewards. My suspicion is that our current reward system is a major producer of the involved struggle, the involved conflict, and politicization in the workplace and, ultimately, of our inability to move on to new world work. The range of rewards offered in most sacrificial situations is extremely limited. Employees rarely hear applause for a job well done. Envious peers play down technical and cultural accomplishments. Bosses often try to take credit for them. Because the intangible rewards gained from doing the job well are largely nonexistent, therefore, all that a majority of us have left to look forward to are the tangible ones, and most of those involve money.

In Chapter 6, then, we will talk about the nature of our current reward system, its origins, its effects on our working and nonworking lives, and, specifically, the dominant role that money plays in it. Only then can we begin to define an alternative that might help free us from "the struggle," from the conflict and political maneuvering we are locked into, and that might help encourage the desired trend toward new world work and real team efforts.

6

WHAT DO WE REALLY WANT?

An organizational reward system can be set up to encourage two things. First, it can encourage employees to fight over the spoils, to try in whatever ways they can think of to increase their share of the loot. Second, it can encourage them to develop their potential as fully as possible and to use that potential to benefit the organization or the team they are a part of as well as themselves. In varying degrees, both types of interaction are usually going on at the same time. The problem is that they do not complement each other, and while the second is obviously more advantageous in terms of at least corporate prosperity, the first is generally where our emphasis lies.

Rewards received for expending our energy at work can take many forms. Most of our current ones, however—especially in the sacrificial type work—are money-based. Though we might experience a sense of pride when the project is completed successfully, the promised raise and promotion are more important. Although a feeling of elation comes when a problem is solved, its the bonus that gives us a real boost. This focus is not producing the desired results. Frequently, in fact, it has a negative effect on the achievement of organizational objectives. Because there is a limited amount of salary available, which has to be divided amongst many, employees tend to fight over it. Our almost exclusively dollar-based incentive system, therefore, is obviously one of the things encouraging conflict. The situation is non-sensical. Yet, currently very little is being done to remedy it. In a way, this traditional means of rewarding people for their efforts has become a sacred cow, a symbol of what we stand for. It has also been glamorized, as in the million-dollar take of top-level executives and the extravagant "perks" sought after.

Money in itself is not a bad thing. It serves a definite purpose in our society. As an extremely tangible and useful reward, it helps us to satisfy many of our needs and desires. Our over-emphasis on and sometimes almost fanatical quest for money, however, can cause great harm. For example, I have read recently about three major corporations that are experiencing serious financial difficulties. All three eventually reshuffled their top-level management teams in an attempt to create a new and more positive atmosphere. The first thing that these newly-formed top-level teams proceeded to do in every case was to announce that employees had to bite the bullet if they wanted to avoid layoffs. Salary freezes, salary cutbacks, and reduction of benefits were all part of the package. The second thing that these new management teams proceeded to do in every case was to give themselves raises or to award themselves bonuses. Their reasoning for this move, I am sure, was that because it is more difficult to turn a company around than to manage one already doing well, those with the final responsibility deserve greater incentive and reward for their efforts. The response to such reasoning is, of course, that most companies get into trouble in the first place due to poor management practices, not because the lower-level employees are slacking off, so that decreasing the rewards of the innocent and increasing those of the guilty might appear a questionable move.

A second example of the negative consequences of our short-sighted quest, just as unrealistic and counter-productive as the first, involves a truck manufacturing firm that also currently is having financial problems. Sales are down. The market is shrinking and the competition is growing increasingly stiff. Previous to this decline, the company had enjoyed a number of good years. During those years the wages of hourly workers rose steadily until it was not uncommon for people to be taking home $20 to $30 an hour including benefits, plus overtime. Everyone, therefore, had profited from the good times. Now the company was asking employees to share in the bad as well and not to ask for another raise.

A majority of those who worked with the company were willing to negotiate, but the national union would not allow them to speak for themselves. It ignored their desires and kept the pressure on for a raise. The union's reasoning was that if it gave in here, unionized companies in other parts of the country might begin making similar demands. As a result of this impasse, the company finally decided to move part of its operation to a southern state, thus eliminating approximately 2,000 jobs at the original site.

Again, the logic of the above chain of events seems weak. We're not talking about a battle for enough to survive. We're not even talking about demanding what is necessary to achieve the good life. What we're talking about at this level of negotiation, instead, is the continuous struggle for more.

The corporate and union worlds are not alone in their frequent lack of perspective. We find this consuming quest for money and the things it can buy everywhere that we look. In the final analysis, very little else seems really to matter to a large percentage of our population. Very little else is taken into consideration when the siren wail of the dollar is heard.

The extent to which our culture has been hypnotized by the dollar was driven home very emphatically to me by a recent personal experience. I frequently walk my dog in a splendid park donated several years ago to our town by a large corporation as part of a deal that gave them the right to locate their corporate headquarters here. The park is approximately 150 acres large and lies in a small valley. At the foot of the valley is a lake. At one end of the lake is a swimming area with a sandy beach. The rest of the well-stocked waters are enjoyed by mallard ducks and fishermen. I have never been there in season without spotting at least half a dozen relaxed-looking sportsmen wading about reeling in flies or standing on the bank casting bait. Pastures of wild golden grass rise up the gently sloping hillsides and edge into a forest of deep green conifers, then hardwood trees. Further along the valley, as it narrows and its sides steepen, a boulder-strewn stream flows, eventually emptying into the lake. Here the forest is thicker, beginning at the stream's edge and climbing past the vine-laced, tumbled stone foundations of century-old, abandoned farm houses.

The park is criss-crossed with well-used walking trails. Bridges built by boy scouts and girl scouts span the stream. Several small waterfalls have carved out clear, pebble-bottomed pools where children hunt crayfish. If one climbs the thickly wooded slopes sliding down to the stream they find shallow caves sheltering the charred embers of camp-fires, and stoney ledges that challenge climbers of all ages.

It is a nice, well-used, well-appreciated recreational area. Frequently one sees a neighbor with a trash bag voluntarily picking up styrofoam cups, cola cans, and other litter forgotten by picnickers or kids who come at night to neck.

I was sitting with a friend in the grass one Saturday afternoon looking down over the lake while our dogs roamed the hillside hunt-ing for scents when two men, probably in their late 30s or early 40s, sat down close by. They were talking excitedly and gesturing, point-ing here and there, so we listened. They were discussing a project to turn the park into a high-class housing development. Apparently, one of them worked for the company that had donated the land and the other was in real estate. The conversation went like this.

"Lake front would go for $300,000. Back it on up the hill, $200,000 halfway, $250,000 to $300,000 on top. Along the stream we could get more creative, terracing. Top-level executive mansions. Big, big bucks. $500,000 by the waterfall. How tight is the agreement?"

"I don't know, but I imagine it would be hard to break."

"You think the company would be interested?"

"I'm not sure they'd think it worthwhile."

"Are you interested?"

"Yes, of course. I'd be glad to invest in something like that."

"This land's too valuable for the town to sit on. I'm not the only one talking this way. Real estate taxes, jobs, corporate taxes. We can make it attractive to the right people. It's going to happen someday, and now's an ideal time with so many corporate headquarters shift-ing out of New York and looking for places to relocate. If we could pull this one off, it would make us."

"There will be a lot of resistance. Lots of groups use this park. My kids have pretty well grown up in it. They'd leave home if they thought I was involved in something like this."

"Don't worry about your kids. Everyone loves a winner. Anyway, there are plenty of other parks around. This is too big a chunk of land to just let sit idle. We could match any development this close in to the city. Once it got rolling, no one would be able to stop it. Too many people would make too much."

At this point my friend turned to them and interrupted, "You're not serious, are you?"

The two men stopped talking and looked at us. "This is a private conversation."

"No, it's not. This park means a lot more to a great number of people in this town than a few extra bucks in someone's pocket."

The two men got up and left. As they walked away the realtor looked back over his shoulder and winked. "We'll see."

When times are tough, money is obviously our major concern. Without it we cannot acquire the things necessary for survival, much less situation improvement. Once our basic needs have been taken care of, however, we must ask ourselves if our continuing quest for more to the exclusion of almost all else is beneficial? Does this quest give us the greatest feeling of personal accomplishment and satisfaction? If there were an ultimate reward, once our survival needs have been taken care of, would it, indeed, be ever increasing amounts of money?

I don't think so. I think that we are confused. We forgot to turn a corner and are wandering around bumping into walls. I think that in terms of "ultimates" there is something that as a society we agree is far more important, once our lives are fairly comfortable—something that money can facilitate the achievement of but that money cannot buy. To me, that something is *respect*. What we want more than anything else in life is respect—self-respect and societal respect. In every culture from the beginnings of recorded history elaborate rituals have been built around the generation and awarding of respect. If we respect a fellow citizen we behave in a certain manner. If we don't we behave in another. One of the first things stressed by groups trying to improve their lot in society, like the Blacks in the United States during the 1960s, is the development of self-respect. We give titles to those who earn our respect, we give awards, we honor them with ceremonies, we add their names to honor rolls, we applaud them, congratulate them, and openly admire them. On the other hand, if we don't respect someone we ignore them, exclude them, say derogatory things about them, and try to make them feel that unless they make the effort necessary to change their image they will never be accepted—a lack of acceptance being perhaps the stiffest punishment a society can deal out.

What we are actually seeking, therefore, with our ever-growing piles of currency appears to be ever-increasing amounts of respect. It is people's *reaction* to our bankroll and acquisitions, rather than the actual amount in our savings accounts or the size of our sailboat, that is important. We work long hours at deadening, sacrificial jobs, not so much for the dollars after a certain level of wealth is reached, but moreso to prove to ourselves and others that we are willing to do what is necessary. This is the reason, I am sure, that Stan panicked when he lost his position, although financial survival was not a problem and was not likely to become one. The issue, instead, had to do with what he saw each morning when he looked in the mirror.

If we can agree, then, that respect, both self and societal, is our modern day ultimate reward we must next realize, as I have indicated above, that self-respect is largely the result of societal respect. We do things that we believe will properly impress those we consider important, whether we know them or not. It's a lot easier to be proud of something we've accomplished when we hear applause. Societal respect, in turn, generally comes when one contributes to the maintenance or improvement of society. The nature of such contributions can vary from culture to culture, but, despite this, what I believe to be a universal standard for judging them has eventually evolved. The standard is very simple. In terms of societal respect, those who earn the most from the greatest number of others are those whose accomplishments benefit the greatest number of others the most.

Using the above as a basis, I can, at this point, define four levels of accomplishments in terms of the amounts of societal and self-respect, in terms of the amount of the ultimate reward they merit. On the top level I would place those accomplishments that improve or lead to the improvement of mankind's general condition. Such accomplishments include important advances in the various fields of human knowledge, as well as glorification of the human spirit and human sensitivities through various forms of artistic expression. In my opinion, Thomas Edison's accomplishments were on this scale, as were Henry Ford's, Walt Disney's, and those of the Wright brothers. The considerable respect paid winners of the Nobel Prize perhaps best exemplifies the esteem in which the world holds such achievements.

On the next lower level of my hierarchy I would place those accomplishments that improve through direct interaction or provision of a service the everyday quality of life for groups of people. Corporate executives who really care about the welfare of their employees, who contribute to the communities in which their operation is located can be credited with such achievements. Teachers, doctors, and other professionals who take their charge seriously are also capable of second-level accomplishments, as well as the sales clerk who is honestly interested in discovering and meeting his customer's needs, the manufacturing team that refuses to cheat the public in terms of quality, the civil servant who makes a sincere effort to understand and deal with the problems brought to him or her, the housewife or househusband who plays an important role in the neighborhood.

On the third level of my hierarchy I would place impressive individual accomplishments. These do not involve direct interaction or the provision of a service. Such accomplishments, instead, provide a respected role model for others to emulate. A current example from the corporate world is Lee Iacocca and the job he has done in helping lead Chrysler back from the edge of bankruptcy. A more traditional one would be the famous baseball player who doesn't do dope, still loves Mom, and knocks the cover off the ball. Other examples are people who might be extremely honest, intelligent, or fearless in the face of danger, like the lady in New York who recently had a crane fall on her, crushing her legs, and who was more concerned about her family than herself. In everyday life we find people who keep a nice flower garden in their front yard, people who love animals, people who always seem to be positive, good natured, and willing to offer a helping hand.

On the fourth and last level of my hierarchy I would place the type of accomplishments we have been talking about in the earlier part of this chapter, those that involve the accumulation of large amounts of money and large numbers of material possessions. A role model again is the result.

Most people can be credited with some number of second-, third-, and fourth-level accomplishments. The critical questions for us, however, at this moment are, "Where do we as a society want the emphasis to lie?" "Where does it, in fact, lie?" and "Why?"

All the world's great religions focus on the top levels. They begin by making gods, saints, and heroes out of individuals capable of first-level accomplishments in the spiritual realm. This group of outstanding contributors includes such well-known figures as Confucius, Buddha, Lao-tzu, Muhammad, Christ, and Moses.

The vast majority of energy expended by every one of these religions, however, is channeled into efforts to guide practitioners toward second- and third-level accomplishments: make a contribution to the community, look out for your brother, give more than you receive. All serious religions also play down fourth-level accomplishments. Wealth can be dangerous if misused. It is a tool for helping improve the human condition; its role is to support first-, second-, and third-level accomplishments. To accumulate it mainly or solely for the purpose of impressing others, however, is unacceptable and wrong. Beyond the church, most of us normally join the boy scouts, the girl scouts, and various other community and service organizations at various stages in our lives, all of which push the same message.

In view of the above, then, it is pretty easy to guess what, as a society, we want our modern-day image to be. We want to be known as tried-and-true "top-downers." We want to be recognized as the nation that cares. This is why, for example, President Kennedy drew such a response when he told us that if we truly want to realize our potential as a nation and as individuals we should think about what we can do for society rather than about what it can do for us.

Very simple. We've heard it many times before. But, as most of us know, it's not working. We certainly give respect to those who make first- and second-level contributions and to those who provide good role models and examples. But in our everyday lives, due to forces largely beyond our control in most cases, a majority of us are unable to practice what we preach. In the corporate world, according to my experience, the only place one finds such language is in corporate mission statements and credos where it reflects the "ideal situation." Progress toward this ideal, however, remains limited by the fact that we are still locked into the fourth level. Monetary rewards generally remain the primary motivation; our emphasis is still on doing what's necessary to win the "prize."

I once was told that in China during the early days of its economic recovery, when someone went into a department store and bought a radio the rest of the customers gathered around and applauded. Because few could afford a radio, those who had earned and saved the necessary amount deserved respect. But what happens when everyone can eventually afford a radio, a TV, a car, to eat out twice a week, and to go on a yearly vacation to Disneyland? Do we continue to escalate the competition endlessly? When does the accumulation of prizes begin to lose meaning in terms of deserving our respect? For example, do we really admire someone who has six cars when they only need one, or who never wears the same shirt twice? Does our applause, at this point, ring true? Or does it come, perhaps, mainly as a conditioned response?

Again, I believe the problem to be primarily one of definition. We are still stuck with a definition and interpretation of rewards that originated long ago. While the environment has changed, our definition of rewards has not. My hypothesis is that the roots of our current reward mentality actually reach back beyond the 16th century, back into the Dark Ages. During that period life was not very pleasant. People enjoyed very little security. The average life expectancy hovered between 30 and 40 years. Disease was rampant. Plague, typhoid, smallpox, dysentery, cholera, tuberculosis, and syphilis were all commonplace. Epidemics periodically swept across Europe, sometimes killing as much as one-third of the total population.

Those who did survive had little to say about their life's course. They served the church and nobility and were used as either or both saw fit. The wealth that did exist was controlled by these two institutions. Commoners were locked into subsistence-level or slave-level jobs with no chance of improving their situation. The ultimate reward, the one most avidly sought during the Dark Ages, was the promise of a decent life after death held out by the church. "Accept the burdens of this existence, do the best that you can, serve the church and your lords faithfully, and paradise will be yours."

This situation remained the status quo until, eventually, technology came to the rescue. A rapidly increasing number of improvements allowed workers to produce a growing variety of products in greater quantities. While during the Dark Ages the only real reward for most had been survival and the degree of emotional uplift gleaned from the church's promised long-term payback, during these later periods improvement of one's immediate circumstances became a real possibility. The increasing amounts of money earnable bought food, shelter, medical attention, and protection from rampaging armies.

This newer reward system seemed much more attractive than that which the church offered. For one thing, it allowed more control. People went for it. Money quickly replaced grace as the number one priority. The mood resulting from these changes helped shape the Industrial Revolution, when technology really came into its own. More and more of the goods and services necessary for a decent life became accessible to the average employee. A satisfactory degree of fourth-level accomplishment became commonplace.

Eventually, especially in parts of western Europe and the United States where economic growth was the most rapid, we reached a stage where we could begin thinking about higher levels of accomplishment. At that point, however, our progress began to falter. The wheels refused to turn. This, then, is where we find ourselves today.

Our 16th century definition of rewards has begun to function as a deterrent to further positive change. It does so in several ways. First, it does so by encouraging a shortage mentality. So long as we continue to measure our success by the number and quality of things we can buy, there will be something that we cannot afford. Therefore, we will persist in seeking ways to win more of the prize so that we can "improve" our situation. Obviously, the competition involved degenerates very quickly into conflict.

Second, it does so by encouraging the ascendency of "politicians" in the workplace. Those whose skills are predominantly technical can be distracted from their pursuit of the prize by the satisfaction that they receive from doing their work well. Those whose skills are predominantly cultural are distracted by the realization that they can successfully coordinate employee efforts and potential in a way that improves organizational performance. Those whose skills are mainly or solely political, however, are well served by our current reward system and its implications. The system plays into their strengths— their ability to manipulate, their willingness to do whatever is necessary. The prize involved is to their liking because it is one that can be gained by those possessing limited technical and cultural skills. At the same time, it is something one can wave under the noses of competitors, saying, "Who cares about what you have to offer? I've won!"

Third, it does so by reinforcing our custom of relating to workers as machine parts. Machines run on one power source, usually electricity. Money, according to this mechanistic way of thinking, should serve as our electricity; it is that which should stimulate workers to perform satisfactorily. The other things critical to successful team efforts and new world work, those that have to do with human as opposed to mechanical interaction, are of secondary importance at best.

Finally, our current definition of rewards thwarts our move to new world work by forcing us to focus on the short-term survival issues that conflict situations continually generate rather than on longer-term developmental ones.

Obviously, at this point, what we need is a new definition of rewards. Obviously, also, we want one that takes into consideration more than just money and the things it can buy. We, as a culture, have begun to realize that money's role must not only be played down, but must also change if we are to progress into an era of new world work. New world work gives us a greater chance at upper-level accomplishments. While we remain locked into sacrificial work, the money earned continues to provide our major and frequently only vehicle for earning the desired respect. Once we start progressing again, however, salary should become just one of several benefits received for our efforts that will help facilitate the development of those capabilities necessary to third-, second-, and first-level accomplishments.

The above statement needs elaboration because it is important. What I am saying is that in order to move on up the hierarchy of accomplishments previously defined, we must develop certain potentials and strengths. The challenge involved necessitates access to a number of critical inputs. One of these, but not necessarily the most important, is an appropriate amount of wealth. While on level four we can directly buy respect, therefore, on any level above that we cannot. Another, intermediate step has been added, as well as the need for additional inputs that we must also begin seeking as part of our reward.

In summary then, the major problem with our current, money-based reward system, as I see it, is that it provides one critical input, but not the only one necessary to true satisfaction of that which we ultimately seek. But exactly what else, then, is necessary? What do we want from our jobs in particular besides money? What kind of reward system would limit conflict and politicization while, at the same time, encouraging an atmosphere that supports developmental activities? What kind of reward system would help transform the typical sacrificial work situation into a new world one? In order to adequately address these questions, we must now come up with two more definitions. The first is a more concise definition of the concept of "development." What, exactly, are the potentials that work should allow and encourage us to realize? The second definition is that of the inputs other than money necessary to the development of those potentials. Have these inputs already been identified? If so, does what has been said before still apply?

These, then, are the two definitions that we will focus on in Chapter 7 as we enter the realm of our third foundational concept, that of overall employment development.

7

A REDEFINED REWARD SYSTEM FOR NEW WORLD WORK

It is obvious by now that as we move into new world work our concept of rewards is being redefined. Salary alone no longer suffices as compensation for the energy we expend. But what, exactly, is it that we seek to gain? What are the capabilities that we want work to give us the opportunity to enhance? What facets of our makeup do we want continually to challenge and strengthen in our efforts to upgrade our level of accomplishment? This is not a new question. It has been asked by many, many thinkers from a great variety of cultures down through the ages. The answers achieved on the most general, all-encompassing level have been pretty much the same. When we talk about the development of individuals and societies, we are talking about four basic but totally interdependent categories of potential: physical, intellectual, emotional, and what I call spiritual, although I do not mean this in the traditional religious sense.

Physical development has to do with improving one's body's strength, endurance, reflexes, and coordination. It results from exercise and training.

Intellectual development is based on learning how to learn. Two things are critical to this effort. The first is that students must learn how to gain access to the necessary information. The second is that they must learn how to process this information and achieve a suitable conclusion. Intellectual development, therefore, is primarily dependent on our learning to do research and on our learning to reason, to think logically.

Emotional development has to do with finding the proper balance between "self" and "other" orientation. It has to do with gaining the necessary understanding of and respect for our own bodies, thoughts, and emotions while at the same time learning to get along with others and to form meaningful relationships.

Spiritual development has to do with putting the rest together to produce a whole person, one who is in tune with and at peace with his or her reality. Spiritually developed individuals are relatively unaggressive, but, at the same time, exert a strong influence on those with whom they interact. Spiritually developed people possess a deep understanding of themselves but at the same time are sensitive to the needs of others. They have a feel for life and seem to know instinctively what the best course of action is. They have developed their potential and in so doing have tapped into some pulse that has eluded the rest of us, offering a full, warm smile and a sense of aliveness that is extremely attractive. Spiritually developed individuals have identified an acceptable purpose in life, one they derive pleasure from, and one that benefits others as well as themselves. Spiritually developed people, therefore, are those capable of creating beauty and harmony in life, either directly through such mediums as music, painting, sculpture, the written word, and acting, or indirectly through the way they interact with others and their environment as a whole, through the example that they set.

This is the additional gain, the additional reward, therefore, that we seek from new world work. We seek the chance to continually develop ourselves physically, intellectually, emotionally, and spiritually, as well as to earn the traditional salary. Our goal is nothing new. We certainly aren't the first culture to define "holistic" individual development as its objective. The Renaissance, or rebirth, period that followed the Dark Ages, for example, was a period during which those with wealth and power eagerly sought to fulfill their potential. Support for the arts during this period came to symbolize the advances being made. The list of valuable artistic contributions made possible by such support is probably as long as that for any period since. The end objective of Renaissance patrons, however, was not only to support, but to actively participate in developmental pursuits themselves. Their aim was to become well balanced, to combine in their makeup physical strength and agility, business acumen, political savvy, artistic talent, scientific prowess, and moral sensitivity. Those thought to have achieved this desired balance eventually were given the title of Renaissance men.

A second, later period during which the topic of human development came to the fore was the Enlightenment. From approximately 1650 to the early 1800s thinkers and leaders became involved not only in self-improvement efforts, but in efforts to provide development opportunity for entire populations. They believed that enough money now existed to provide wealth-based security for all people, at least in the "civilized" Western world. Men like Jean-Jacques Rousseau theorized that, using this wealth-based security as a launching pad, entire populations could now reach the desired level of holistic development and achievement. The major purpose of such thinkers was to make possible a new world order and to create a social mechanism that would allow everyone to contribute fully to the maintenance of that order.

Thinkers of both the Renaissance and the Enlightenment periods, in their search for a foundation upon which to build their developmental efforts, used the findings of the ancient Greek philosophers mentioned earlier as a major resource. It is my belief that we will end up doing the same. In our quest for a modern day *development ethic*, the ethic we are slowly fashioning to replace our current *work ethic*, we will eventually also turn to the Greeks for guidance.

Another belief I harbor is that we are currently in a position to combine the strengths of the Renaissance with those of the Enlightenment in order to achieve a truly systemic development model. We can combine the Renaissance's focus on individual definition with the Enlightenment's quest for a society-wide implementation mechanism and come up with something that really works. One of the factors supporting this belief is the amount of wealth we now have at our disposal. While during the Enlightenment the premise that enough existed to provide everyone with an acceptable degree of wealth-based security was largely wishful thinking, today it is fact. As a result of our continuing technological progress, every person can, indeed, be a "merchant prince" capable of realizing his or her potential. Also, due at least partially to our tremendous advances in the field of communications, we are capable of constructing the societal mechanisms necessary to the universal distribution of developmental opportunities.

With that said, my next question must obviously be, "How are we doing so far, folks? How does our society's level of development compare with that of the other historical periods discussed?" The answer must be, of course, "Not so good." We don't seem to be making that much progress. In some areas, in fact, we seem to be going backward.

In order to elaborate, let's talk first about our physical development. As a nation, unfortunately, we have been out of shape for a long time. We have produced some of the best individual athletes and teams that the world has ever known, but on a societal basis we have either ignored or taken this critical area for granted. One proof of my statement is the fact that during most of our wars recruiters have had trouble finding enough physically fit men to fill the ranks and eventually have been forced to lower their standards. Another source of proof is the current cluster of reports telling us that our children are in poor physical condition. One simply has to visit the local supermarket and watch overweight mothers rolling their roly-poly little kids up and down the aisles of sodas and cookies and potato chips and candy in their shopping carts to gain some feel for how serious this problem is.

On the positive side I see two promising trends. One is our nation's growing emphasis on proper nutrition. Health food stores and health food aisles in the grocery markets are booming. The second trend is the apparent national movement toward physical fitness that goes beyond simply wearing the most expensive running shoes and designer jogging outfit. Yoga and exercise classes appear daily on television; health clubs seem to be flourishing. People are out there working up a sweat. The major problem seems to be one of time. Almost half our waking hours are spent at work. The rest must be divided among activities and responsibilities that seem to increase in number as we grow older. We frequently just don't have the time necessary to exercise properly.

But what about the world of work where we spend so many of our potentially productive hours? How does this world feel about physical development? The good news is that the corporate world, at least, seems to be embracing the fitness trend. Cafeterias now cater to the desires of those wary of cholesterol, calories, sugar, and caffeine. Weight-watcher and exercise clubs are spring up. Growing numbers of health-related materials are being circulated or posted on bulletin boards. The bad news is my suspicion that most such efforts are largely reactions to studies showing that healthy employees are more productive. Emphasis, in terms of physical development, therefore, remains on improving the bottom line and on increasing stockholders' wealth rather than on helping individuals realize their true physical potential as part of their reward for helping the corporation achieve its objectives.

One clear indication that my suspicions are correct is the nature of the exercise facilities movement. Very few corporate visits that I have made during the past few years as a consultant have not eventually included a tour of these facilities. A majority of such tours have occurred during working hours. With this in mind, the thing that has impressed me the most, in every case, has not been the quality and abundance of equipment. Rather, it has been the fact that no one was using it. Employees like Brian in our Chapter 1 scenario are generally allowed to use corporate exercise facilities before work begins, during lunch hour, and after work. I have rarely heard of a boss who took the time to help his or her staff generate a during-hours workout schedule. The impression given is that everyone is far too busy to spare the time, and if they aren't, they should be.

In the corporate world, therefore, our perspective concerning the value of physical development is still extremely narrow. We do not take the positive benefits to both the individual and the corporation seriously enough. At the same time, we seem to accept as givens some of the more negative aspects of our current work life. I would guess, for example, that over 50 percent of the jobs in our business sector involve sitting most of the day at a desk, a computer terminal, a typewriter, or a control panel. Sitting in one place for long periods of time is detrimental to our health in general. Our posture gets worse. We lose our muscle tone. We grow pot bellies and large, flabby bottoms. Ways exist, of course, to create a healthier environment. Some cultures, for example, have made group exercise sessions an integral part of their work schedule. Encouraging people simply to get up and walk around occasionally helps. Although such improvements sound simple in terms of implementation, they are not. I learned this one beautiful fall day several years ago when I suggested that a small meeting I had set up at a corporate headquarters be held on the building's spacious, empty front lawn. "Let's walk while we talk," I said, "or at least while we sit in the sunshine. It might inspire us."

At first those present thought that I was kidding. When they eventually realized that I was, indeed, serious, they shook their collective head. "Can't be done."

"Why not?" I asked.

"No blackboard."

"We'll carry out a flipchart," I said.

"No telephone. I'm expecting a call."

"Someone can carry a portable," I countered.

"Too many distractions."

Just then a secretary barged in with something that had to be signed.

Finally, we got down to what I think was the truth of the matter. "Too many windows. People would see us and wonder what the hell we're doing walking around out there instead of sitting in a conference room where we belong." The issue, it turned out, was once again our old friend the work ethic. My associates were afraid to do something that smacked of self-gratification, no matter how appealing, no matter how beneficial the results might be in terms of our meeting's objectives.

The encouragement of intellectual development should be a strong point in our culture. We probably have access to more information than any other modern-day society. There seem to be endless avenues of knowledge to venture down. Indeed, perhaps the major problem that we face today in this area is how best to bound our inquisitiveness. How do we decide what's really important? How do we sort through the deluge of newspaper print, magazine articles, books, TV, and radio reports and put together the collection of information that best suits our individual needs? Our culture's weak point in terms of intellectual development is providing skills necessary to absorb and successfully manipulate all this information. According to the reports that I have been reading, an apparently increasing percentage of our population lacks them.

From the corporate world the good news is that intellectual development is being pushed hard. Almost all corporations now offer educational benefits. These range from company-run courses in basic skills for employees who didn't learn what they were supposed to before beginning to work, to computer and other technical training programs, to management skills training, to reimbursement for college and graduate courses and degrees. The bad news from the developmental perspective is that the range of subjects employees are allowed to study, in most cases, is extremely limited. Courses have to be job related. Companies rarely encourage the pursuit of other interests that might indirectly also greatly enhance performance. Emphasis, therefore, is again mainly on improving the bottom line rather than on improving the corporate reward system and contributing to the creation of a better all-around employee.

Another problem in the intellectual realm is again time. The company provides reimbursement, but courses must usually be taken on the employee's own time. Thus, intellectual development must compete with physical development and other activities and responsibilities for one's daily free hours. I have taught working MBAs. They were easily the best overall students that I have ever had. It has been rather unsettling, however, to sometimes watch them fight to stay awake for the duration of a three-hour class after an eight- or nine-hour day in the office and no dinner.

In terms of emotional development our society does not seem to be doing that well. Perhaps it is because we have not really "jelled" yet. Perhaps it is the constant tensions we live with as a major power in a nuclear world at so young and tender an age. Perhaps it is because our traditional family structure is breaking down. Perhaps its due to all the violence and perversion we see on television and in the movies. Perhaps it's the easy access we have to drugs, often beginning in early childhood. There are many, many possibilities. The point is that, despite the increasing amounts of help available for mental health problems, things don't seem to be improving that rapidly, if at all.

The corporate world isn't doing much better than the rest. It has taken a stab at this issue, but emphasis is still on doing what's necessary to make sure that employees show up for work in the morning. Many companies now offer discrete counselling for drug addiction and alcoholism. Some provide help for other emotional problems as well. Consultants are brought in to improve communication among employees and to identify and break down interpersonal barriers. Executives attend courses like Eslon that encourage them to relax and regain a more balanced perspective. True to our work ethic tradition, however, and conflict mentality, emphasis remains on being tough and aggressive. Those who admit they have doubts, that they are not yet "together" and have problems that must be addressed before they can find any peace are often perceived as being weak and not cut out for the "big time." Encouraging the realization of emotional potential, it seems, in the true developmental sense is not yet a serious consideration in the corporate world and is certainly not an objective of our corporate reward system.

In terms of spiritual development, then, or that which pulls the rest together into a well-balanced, purposeful whole, due to the absence of the required degree of physical, intellectual, and emotional development, our society has not yet really gotten off the ground. We talk about spiritual development at cocktail parties, we read about it on the train and before going to sleep at nights, but it still remains at least part fantasy, part joke. Our thinking is still too fragmented. We do not yet understand how such a generalistic perspective, or one that concentrates on balance rather than on the cultivation of one well-defined strength, could allow us to flourish, much less survive in our current turbulence-riddled reality. In the corporate world we have not yet found the time even to discuss such matters seriously on most levels lower than that of the presidency.

When we put all the above together it becomes fairly obvious that our efforts to achieve overall human development are not going as well as we might desire. With this realization in mind, our next question must be, "Why not? Why, in this land of so much opportunity are we not moving right along?" The answer is that we are not "moving right along" because the *inputs* necessary to the realization of our physical, intellectual, emotional, and spiritual capabilities are not always available, or when they are available their price is frequently too high or their value is suspect.

But what exactly are these inputs we've been talking about? In Chapter 3, for example, we discussed our general need for both continuity in terms of those things important to our security, and change. We have also spoken of our need for control in life. But what, for example, constitutes continuity? What inputs are necessary to the maintenance of an acceptable and comfortable routine? Again, what constitutes our general need for change? What inputs allow us to enjoy the stimulation and challenge defined as desirable? Finally, how do we, indeed, gain the critical degree of control over the rest? What inputs help ensure that we achieve the required access?

Quite a few attempts have been made to identify the full range of inputs important to development. In the Western world, however, it is once again the Greeks who seem to have given us our soundest and most well-thought-out, all-encompassing model. Of the ancient Greek philosophers and teachers who held forth on the subject, Aristotle produced the work that ultimately had the most impact. Aristotle said that life has three primary dimensions: making, doing, and knowing. With these three dimensions in mind, he then identified four basic types of inputs critical to human development: those related to wealth, knowledge, morality, and aesthetics.

Russell Ackoff has updated these categories and related them to our current situation. He says that the individual and societal pursuit of four ideals—or inputs that can never be fully achieved—is critical to modern-day development. These four ideals are plenty, truth, good, and beauty. Jamshid Gharajedaghi has added a fifth to the list, that of power. Although we find no correlate in Aristotle's system to the ideal of power, I agree that its pursuit is also critical to holistic individual and societal development.

Ackoff's pursuit of plenty involves the quest for a steady supply of those things necessary to our wealth-based security. The acquisition of plenty is obviously a result of fourth-level achievements. Ackoff's pursuit of truth includes efforts to gain the knowledge necessary to the selection and achievement of desirable work and leisure time objectives. His pursuit of good has to do with our desire for assurances that a fair deal will be received, that we will be given credit when credit is due, and will not be victimized by those with more power. The last of Ackoff's ideals is beauty. The pursuit of beauty concerns our quest for contentment and excitement in life, contentment resulting from a pleasing, nonthreatening work and leisure environment that sooths the senses; excitement resulting from the availability of challenge, newness, and adventure that stimulate the senses.

Finally, we have the pursuit of Gharajedaghi's ideal input of power, which, I believe, is similar to our desire for control. Power over the sources of plenty, truth, good, and beauty in our lives is critical. Without it, we will never be able to relax completely. Also, we will not be quite as willing to take the needs of others into consideration.

The matchup between our initial needs framework and Aristotle's, Ackoff's, and Gharajedaghi's ideal inputs seems to be very neat. Continuity in terms of those things necessary to our security results largely from adequate supplies of plenty and good. We need a reasonable amount of income along with assurances that no one can disrupt our life pattern without our approval. Change that provides stimulation and challenge comes largely from learning or the pursuit of truth and the aesthetics of our lives, or the pursuit of beauty. We need continual access to the new and different, as well as an environment that appeals to our senses. Finally, the control we consider so critical in all areas comes only with the acquisition of the necessary amount of power. The best way to keep from being planned for is by gaining the ability to do our own planning.

With this said, my next question must be, once again, "How are we doing, folks?" in terms of generating these necessary inputs? And once again, the response must be, "Not so good, I'm afraid." This time I am going to focus entirely on the access corporate employees have to plenty, truth, good, beauty, and power, for the free enterprise sector, as we have said, is the key to positive change in our society. It will lead the way.

In terms of plenty, our first requisite input, enough obviously exists to facilitate on-the-job developmental efforts. Proof of this claim includes the well-equipped corporate exercise facilities being put into place, the wide range of educational benefits being made available to almost every employee, and the social and emotional services that seem to be growing in number and quality.

In terms of truth, or access to the information necessary to turn one's job into a worthwhile learning experience, we have not been so fortunate. The problem is not that the desired or required information is lacking in the environment. The corporate world is awash with it. The problem, rather, is that due to the conflict mentality we have been talking about and the political atmosphere, critical information is frequently made inaccessible to those who need or desire it. Lee Iacocca in his autobiography talked about the "cluster of little duchies" he found at the top level of management when he arrived at Chrysler, "thirty-five vice presidents each controlling his own turf" with minimal communication and sharing of information between them (p. 152). This situation is not unusual. Management consultants know automatically when they are called into a company that the initial problem they will have to address, no matter what the client says, most frequently will be the lack of process-oriented communication among divisions, departments, levels, and individuals. Management consultants also know that once they get people talking and information flowing freely through the organization, many of the other problems will disappear. In terms of truth, then, the attitudes and vehicles necessary to give us unrestricted access to it in most corporate situations are still lacking.

In terms of good, the frequent emphasis on expediency found in corporations makes a fair shake rather difficult to assure. One of the key problems in this realm is our traditional emphasis on the numbers. Management's on-going love affair with the quantitative appraisal of situations began approximately in the late 1800s when Frederick Taylor introduced scientific management. His purpose with this approach was to help bring rapidly growing industries under control. His means was to develop formulas, measurements, and standards for as many production-related processes as possible. Managers learned to like what Taylor was doing. They quickly realized that numbers were much easier to manipulate than multifaceted employees.

As time passed and corporations continued to grow, our dependency on this approach increased. With thousands of employees now involved, it became more and more difficult to take individual personalities and needs into account when making decisions. Also, Wall Street began putting increased amounts of dollar or "numbers related" pressure on companies. Wall Street also began demanding increasing amounts of the CEO's time and attention, until today we have corporate heads who rarely, if ever, visit and have no real interest in visiting production facilities. Their role, as they see it, is to safeguard the financial security of their organization and to stave off attacks from above, such as attempted buyouts. They feel obligated to do whatever is necessary with the numbers in order to protect the future of the operation, even though a large percentage of those numbers represent people. The end result of this reasoning is that everyone is expendable if their "number comes up." There is no protection. Performance, for example, is not usually a serious consideration, especially at the lower levels, when it comes time to cut costs. Seniority is frequently a detriment because more experienced employees draw higher salaries and, therefore, are worth more in terms of savings—in terms of the "numbers." Until the above situation changes, then, access to good in the corporate world will remain extremely tenuous.

In terms of beauty, we again find shortcomings. As I wend my way through the modern corporate office complex, usually a hodgepodge of little cells connected by narrow, divider-lined alleys, I frequently feel as though I should be squeaking and looking for a piece of cheese. Efficiency is what it is all about. We have somehow misplaced the realization that by sacrificing a few inches or feet in order to make the environment more pleasant, we might actually benefit productivity as well as employee moral. When buildings and offices occasionally do show some flair in terms of their arrangement and decor, the changes wrought rarely are a reflection of the tastes of those who must work in them. Experts have been hired to decorate, or the president's wife has taken the task upon herself. What hangs on your office walls or grows in your plant stand, therefore, is not really "you."

An extreme but not unusual example of such depersonalization and desire to exclude the aesthetic as a distraction was related to me by a corporate director whose office was on the 37th floor of a Chicago skyscraper. He had a large picture window from which he could see the lake on a clear day, but his desk faced in the other direction. One afternoon he decided to turn the desk around so that he could take advantage of the view. The next morning the desk was back in its original position. Being a somewhat reckless soul, he turned it again. The next morning it was back in its original position. He decided to try once more, but this time he turned it only halfway. The next morning the desk was back in its original position and a message lay on his blotter explaining that he should stop bucking corporate policy and that his attitude had been noted.

In terms of power, a majority of those in sacrificial work situations do not enjoy very much. The lack of overall employee participation in problem solving and decision making, and the lack of appropriate incentives are the two main obstacles. It is only through teamwork, as we have said, that the kind of power beneficial to both individual and group development is generated. When the team is large enough and includes enough representatives from enough layers, it eventually begins running the show in a way that benefits everyone with a stake in the outcome.

In summary, then, as soon as we can move beyond money as our major and frequently only reward for work, and begin earning true access to the other inputs critical to individual and societal development as well, we should be able to leave conflict and the age of the politician behind and progress more rapidly toward an era of new world work. In order to move beyond our infatuation with money, however, there is one more related obstacle to surmount beyond our clinging to the work ethic, our misinterpretation of technology's value, our inability to shake the conflict mentality, our acceptance of a politicized workplace, and our slowness in defining and in- corporating into our thinking the basics of human and societal development—one which I believe needs to be discussed. It is the result of another bad habit related to the above and powerful enough also to demand a radical shift in perception. This obstacle is our continuing emphasis on image as opposed to content, on appearances as opposed to performance. It is the obstacle that I shall discuss in Chapter 8.

8

THE SEARCH FOR
A BETTER BALANCE

We are all located somewhere on what I call the "image-content scale."
Our location helps define our approach to the achievement of self-
and societal respect. It shows how much we depend on appearances,
or image, and how much we depend on our performance, or content,
in our quest for this ultimate reward.

During our early years, emphasis is normally on image. In terms of
clothing, for example, when I was a kid, the objective was to wear
the same thing everyone else wore. During high school days this was
usually chino pants, white socks, and white duck shoes. I clearly
remember the white ducks because they were so difficult to keep
clean. I had to stop every few minutes and pat them with a small bag
of white powder, especially when friends "accidentally" stepped on
them, grinding their heel down into my toe.

When I reached the age of 16, access to a car, no matter how old
or beat up, became critical. The ultimate disgrace was to have a rival
drive past with a full load of friends and honk when you were on foot.
My desire was to create the proper impression so that my peers would
accept me. In order to do so I had to meet certain dress, speech,
activity, interest, and even sometimes motion requirements. Fortu-
nately, at this point, the necessary props were generally affordable.

As I matured, however, my perspective gradually began to shift.
I eventually started to think more about content issues, about the

whys behind my desired image, about what these whys meant in terms of my own personal needs and development. Such changes were encouraged by books or films that electrified me at some vulnerable moment. One such book that I remember was Hermann Hesse's *Siddhartha*. A film, for some reason, was "The Big Country."

Another force pushing me toward content issues was the increasingly persistent inquiries from my parents concerning what I wanted to *do* with my life. Such probes most frequently hit me at the dinner table when the topic of college came up. "You must, by now, have some idea. What do you want to *be*?" I came up with lots of answers to these persistent queries, though I was pretty sure none of them were *the* answer. Too many mysteries remained unsolved for me at this stage in my life to pinpoint *the* answer. My uncertainty, however, did not stop me from packing my bags and moving on into the exciting, glamorous world of higher education, where life proved even more complex. There appeared to be a far greater abundance of alternatives to choose from than I had previously suspected. It was here that I reached that juncture at which it was time to make my first critical choice between an image and content orientation.

It was obviously easiest, at least in the short run, to stick with image. All one had to do was to continue the now familiar practices of youth—identifying fads or trends in their early stages, acquiring the appropriate "impression pieces," learning the necessary buzz words and facts, and surrounding oneself with other appreciative, image-oriented people. At the same time, however, if one chose to stick with the image world, to make a career of it, a new, critical dimension that reshaped the rules was emerging. The necessary props—designer clothes, sports cars, rare wines, sophisticated sound systems, vacations in exotic places—were growing more expensive. Affluence, therefore, was becoming an increasingly important, if not the most important, ingredient to "success."

If one chose, instead, to shift his or her perspective away from image, to attempt to slide down the scale toward the content end, he or she frequently began running into difficulties almost immediately. The adjustment was not easy. For one thing, image challenges kept popping up and competing fiercely for attention. For the people who persisted, however, goals and objectives were chosen increasingly for their value in terms of what they had identified as their developmental requirements. When content-oriented people that I have known decided on a vocation or job, their choice was usually based more on what they'd be doing and on what they could learn than on the salary and perks they could demand. When content-oriented people acquired possessions or even companions, the possessions or companions were chosen more because of their ability to make life more interesting and fuller than for their ability to impress.

For example, a friend of mine, an extremely content-oriented physicist, once told me a story about his years with the old Philco Corporation. Eventually, he had been promoted into the ranks of upper-level management. The big surprise came the day after his promotion when he arrived at his assigned parking place and found a new Cadillac there. The president and vice-presidents were waiting for him in his office and, after some kidding, announced that the company had bought him the car to help him fit more comfortably into his new position. The old jalopy he drove was obviously no longer appropriate.

My friend had been embarrassed. The old jalopy had served him well as a second car, getting him back and forth to work, carrying him on errands. It had needed little maintenance. He hadn't needed to worry about scratching it up. It was a good car for the kids to drive, and it had left him room in the garage for a workbench. Now he had to pay more for insurance and gas, worry about accidents or vandalism, worry about his kids getting swelled heads, and find a new place for his workbench. The whole thing had made little sense to him.

Image-centered people do things for the sake of status. They need to attract attention, to be able to compare impression pieces, and to win their endless one-upmanship battles. A certain amount of image-oriented activity is normal, even healthy, especially when we are younger. When it is overdone, however, problems can arise. The most severe of these problems is experienced when individuals become so image-oriented that they begin judging everyone, as well as everything, that they touch in terms of impression piece value. For example, I am sure that we all have known both men and women who present their wives, girlfriends, husbands, and boyfriends mainly as impression pieces, discussing their attributes as they would those of a new rider mower being shown off. The objective of such presentations obviously is not to applaud the mate's accomplishments. Rather, it is to flaunt one's own ability to find and afford such a gem as this. Such people pick a partner, not because he or she has shown or is developing potential that excites or attracts. Rather, they pick the partner that is superficially the most "right." The winner displays the right manners, dresses the right way, speaks with the right intonation, drops the right names. The fact that he or she might be an individual with something extraordinary to offer physically, intellectually, emotionally, or spiritually is of secondary importance. Frequently, in fact, such potential is seen as a threat. The mate's predefined purpose is to make the image-oriented person look good.

The above type of relationship is relatively unfair and unproductive in terms of development. The good news is that an adult can usually walk away from it if he or she gets fed up. Things get more serious, however, when the impression-piece mentality begins shaping a parent's relationship with his or her children. The tell-tale line, spoken or unspoken, is, "In order to please me, darling, you must win this Little Miss Kindergarten Beauty Contest, or gain admission to an Ivy League school, or become the best running back in the state, or not get your clothes dirty while playing because people will wonder what kind of parents we are." There is insufficient consideration for the child's need to begin figuring things out, to begin making his or her own decisions based on steadily improving judgement, self-understanding, and self-confidence. The role of such children is, again, to make parents look good. They spend their earlier years trying desperately to do what is necessary to earn the desired love and their later years trying desperately to figure out who they are, or who they might have become if they had been given the right kind of support by their parents.

Content-centered people are less interested in status and more interested in discovering, developing, and exercising their individual potential. They learn from others whenever possible but compete mainly with themselves, continually setting higher and higher personal standards to strive for. Concerning our hierarchy of accomplishments that bring societal and self-respect, then, people who have reached level one, those capable of feats that benefit the totality of humanity, usually reside at the content end of the scale. The amount of understanding required to make an intellectual or intuitive contribution of this magnitude requires a great deal of self-knowledge as well as intense concentration. Such intensity usually precipitates a loss of interest in one's immediate environment. The absent-minded professor myth may well be rooted in reality. A first-level contribution, however, also necessitates a clear, concise perception of reality so that the understanding developed is accurate. It seems that first-level achievers are, indeed, open to what is going on about them, but have become true "why" seekers. They have learned to focus on the reasons behind what they see, rather than just on what they see. They work their way through the image part to get at the essence, to get to the content part.

People on the second and third levels of the accomplishment hierarchy, those whose activities benefit groups and those who provide role models, are usually the most balanced in terms of the scale. Image and content both play important roles in their lives. They can, of course, lean toward one or the other extreme and frequently do so at different stages in their careers.

People on the fourth level are usually image oriented. Their energies have been spent mainly on collecting "impression pieces." They seem to have little real interest in content issues. Content is more difficult to flash. Also, you can't buy it. The required investment is largely one of time, effort, and patience, rather than dollars. People on the fourth level, therefore, depend mainly or totally on their acquisitions to gain them the desired societal and self-respect.

The next question is, where do we, as a society, lie on the image-content continuum? My belief is that we lie toward the image end. But why so? Most of the purely image people I have met have been, in the final analysis, unsatisfied. They have identity problems. They have, in essence, become designer jeans, or a sports car, or a large expense account. That's how people describe them. That's how they frequently describe themselves. They have been so busy keeping up that they haven't taken the time necessary to discover and adequately nurture an individualized emotional identity.

The single-minded quest for image, it turns out, keeps us informed and up to date. But it rarely makes us wiser. Neither does it make us stronger as personalities nor more sensitive to ourselves and others. Also, it does not facilitate communication with people from whom we can learn. Frequently, in fact, it has just the opposite effect. It makes us defensive, envious, and suspicious. Why, then, do we persist?

The answer, I believe, has several parts. The first has to do with the old days that we continually refer to as the source of our current problems, with the Dark Ages when shortages of almost everything except suffering existed. Someone who possessed a well-rounded belly back then or who was seen sitting down daily to a table stacked with food obviously enjoyed a superior life style. Those who walked through the village streets with a warm cloak wrapped around their shoulders or lived in a soundly-built house with glass windows, shutters, and a chimney were better off in terms of the essentials.

Because the possession of certain basic types and amounts of material goods is normally a prerequisite to human development, appearances during these earlier periods of deprivation told the true tale in terms of a person's level of developmental achievement. When you looked at someone, you could tell by their physical state, their dress, their horse, their entourage what their chances of surviving and of leading a full life were.

In today's technologically-advanced societies, as we have said, a vast majority of the population has gained access to these basics and to much more. Yet, we continue to judge development by appearances. While huge food surpluses exist, at least in the United States, while people periodically clean out their clothes closets to make way for new wardrobes, while relatively few lack decent housing, we still depend on appearance as our measure of one's level of success.

It is again chiefly a matter of societal habit. Our situation has changed, but our thinking and definitions have not. As I indicated in Chapter 6, we are currently confusing development with excessive materialism. Besides habit, however, I believe that there might also be a second, more subtle reason for this on-going love affair with conspicuous consumption, as the 19th century U.S. sociologist and economist Thorstein Veblen labeled it. This second reason has to do with our continuing pride in and awe of modern man's accomplishments. We are still celebrating our victory over hunger, disease, and cold. Every time we buy an unnecessary trinket, we are patting ourselves on the back. Every time we spend lavishly during a night out on the town we are saying, "Hey, look at us. We did it!" It is almost instinctive. Even those who are still poor seem sometimes to appreciate this sort of display, and not in a totally envious way.

A third reason for our current situation is the effectiveness of one of our most powerful economic sub-institutions. This is the advertising industry, or "Madison Avenue." Advertising originated as a means of letting people know what products were available. The advent of department store catalogues, for example, revolutionized the selling game. We had developed the manufacturing systems necessary to meet an increasing number of the population's needs and desires. Coupled with this, we now needed ways to attract people's attention and get them to spend their money.

As the years passed the unlimited market disappeared and companies had to begin competing for customers, first on a local, then on a national and eventually international basis. Advertising techniques, by necessity, grew increasingly sophisticated. Psychologists began doing studies on how to get people to notice and remember a specific product, differentiating it from the rest of the growing barrage of slogans, colors, shapes, and sounds filtering into every crevice of our awake, and sometimes our asleep, lives.

The emphasis of advertising also shifted during this period from simply letting people know what goods and services were available toward encouraging potential customers to buy. In terms of buying, the most critical objective became not to convince the public to purchase this or that car, this can of tomato sauce instead of that one. Rather, it became to condition potential customers simply to buy. Buying became the answer to all our problems. Health could be bought if you could afford a special piece of exercise equipment. Happiness could be bought if you could afford a pale blue telephone or a new home with triple-pane windows. Acceptance could be bought if you could afford the right labels on your clothing or to drink the right lager beer. A feeling of security could be bought if you put your savings with the right investment group.

Madison Avenue learned to play skillfully on and reinforce the self-doubts and loneliness that we all sometimes feel. It offered quick, miracle cures. It also learned the value of perpetual motion. It told us that we couldn't afford to wait, we had to rush from one fad to the next. "Don't hesitate. Don't take the time to evaluate, or you might miss out on something critical. The only *real* requirement to eventual success is that you have enough cash in your pockets to go on buying."

The world of advertising, obviously, is largely fourth-level oriented in terms of our hierarchy of respected accomplishments. Most advertising agencies focus their energies on reinforcing the belief that image, and the material goods and services that make up image, are the ingredients most important to self-respect and development. They pay relatively little attention to content. The image market is more lucrative. It offers a much greater diversity of products around which to build campaigns. Account managers find it much easier to produce copy on a fragrant, sensual, amber-colored perfume than on a good, thought-provoking book.

Our continuing fixation with image or appearances is nowhere more obvious than in the corporate setting. Perhaps, again, this is because work is frequently so unrewarding otherwise. But that answer is too simple. There has to be more involved. Many of those running our business world seem to be suffering from some form of self-hypnosis. This possibility was forcefully brought to my attention by a friend's story. My friend works in a corporate finance department. He has good technical skills but possesses limited cultural skills and extremely limited political skills. As a result of this imbalance he is reputed to be somewhat "spacey." Like Brian in Chapter 1, my friend commutes daily into New York City from a suburb. He told me that the commute last winter seemed colder than usual. The temperature was frequently in the 20s, the wind whipping through the glass-walled city canyons as he walked the last couple of blocks to his office, driving the huddled masses before it. My friend happens to own a pair of large and very tender ears that smart sharply when they get cold. To minimize his discomfort he always wears the warmest hat he can find. Last winter he said that his choice was a double-knit blue ski cap that he could pull way down to protect the back of his neck as well.

One day in the middle of December his closest companion at work, an old-timer named Stu who was helping him to "get with the program," came into his office, a very serious look on his face. "Bob," he announced, "You've got to stop it."

"Stop what?" my friend had asked in puzzlement.

"That hat. You've got to stop wearing that hat. People are talking. You're beginning to get a reputation as an eccentric, and that's bad."

"But my ears get cold," my friend had protested.

Stu had frowned. "That's not the point, Bob. Just do me a favor and look around tomorrow. At least take it off before you come into the building."

The next day Bob had looked around. He had looked around on the train. Almost no one had hats on. He had looked around when he disembarked at Grand Central Terminal. After sweeping through the lobby with the great, thundering herd and up the marble stairs to the Lexington Avenue exit, he had broken away and stood on the balcony beside the bar gazing down on a sea of bobbing, bare heads. When he reached his own building he had stopped at the top of the escalator to look around one more time. Almost all the people coming up had been topless in the nontraditional sense. The temperature display on the bank wall across the street had read 26 degrees. The wind had been driving fiercely up Park Avenue, yet almost no one Bob had seen that morning was wearing a hat.

My friend had been unable to believe it. There were only two possibilities. First, everyone else was crazy. Second, he had been issued a pair of defective ears. Here they were, the highest-paid executives in the world, the brains behind the most powerful, successful, pragmatic, innovative economic sector ever put together, and they didn't have enough sense to bring their ears in out of the cold.

Of course, that wasn't true. At home I'm sure most of the people my friend had seen that morning did wear hats. They had worn them while sweeping the sidewalk, while taking their dog for its evening stroll, while building a snowman with the kids. What had happened was that somehow, at some point in corporate history, they had been convinced or had convinced themselves that the necessary "going-to-work-in-the-morning" image did not include a hat, no matter how cold it grew, and from that time on, ears had become second-class citizens.

While the subservience to our image impulses illustrated by my friend's story ended up harming no more than a few thousand or hundred thousand pairs of innocent ears, things get more serious when image or appearances remain the most important consideration once we are seated behind our desks. Obviously such a mindset can be counterproductive to long-term corporate objectives. We spoke earlier of busy work, which is a relatively mild manifestation of the appearance syndrome. It results partially from and encourages the pressures generated by a conflict atmosphere in sacrificial work. Less mild manifestations resulting from and encouraging these same pressures are found in the daily activities of most corporations and take a more direct and serious toll in terms of productivity.

For example, I once worked on a consulting project in a metal fabricating plant. The purpose of the project was to find ways to involve hourly employees more thoroughly in productivity improvement efforts. Part of our approach was to form area teams and to help these teams identify things they could do to improve the quality of the operation within their own area of expertise. It rapidly became obvious that one of the chief issues was waste and that a major cause of the waste involved was over-emphasis on tidiness. Whenever word came down that people from corporate headquarters were scheduled to visit, orders went out to clean up the place. If a machine had been torn apart for repair and the parts were lying about, main-

tenance personnel were supposed to rush the job and get it back together. If they couldn't reassemble the machine in time, they were
supposed to hide the parts. The main hiding place for unsightly parts
was the junk heap. According to team members, thousands of dollars
worth of perfectly good materials were periodically thrown away in
this manner. When the panic was over, instead of taking the time to
recover and clean up the old parts, employees would simply order a
new supply from the stock room.

Corporate executives and staff members visited this plant on a
rather steady basis because it was one of the most productive in the
system. Two types of visitors arrived. The first type included those
who had never worked in a plant, had only a superficial understanding of the involved manufacturing process, and didn't really care
much about what was going on. Their visits were usually problem
specific so that only one small part of the operation received their
attention. The second type of visitor included people who had come
up in the metal fabrication industry and knew intimately the systems involved. They understood that the major activity in plants was
not fabrication but maintenance. Disassembling machines was a
normal part of the daily routine.

The stress on tidiness and its cost in terms of waste was, therefore,
largely unnecessary. What had probably happened at some point was
that a visitor of the first type had seen enough to come away with
the impression that it was messy, wondering out loud at corporate
headquarters how the employees got anything done, why they didn't
have more accidents, how they avoided waste with so many materials
lying around. Word of this indictment had filtered down to the plant
manager, as it always does, and the plant manager had instinctively
put more stress on maintaining at least the appearance of neatness.

As the order to clean up had passed down through the chain of
command and exaggeration had occurred, as it always does, so that
by the time it reached the shop floor one division superintendent, at
least, took it so seriously that he had discontinued a program encouraging hourly workers to cross-train during their slack periods and
instead put brooms in their hands to sweep up, no matter how many
times the floor had already been swept that day, just to make sure
they were ready.

A second workplace trend we have talked about that again partially
results from and encourages our emphasis on appearances is politicization. As we have said, politicians are big on appearances. A modern-

day example of what happens when a politician is in control can be taken from the current quality improvement movement. Quality improvement efforts are nothing new. They have been going on in other countries for years, even decades. Japan, Sweden, Poland, and Germany have shown the way. In the United States, more recently, corporations and divisions of companies such as Alcoa, Proctor and Gamble, Kodak, and Ford have received recognition for their programs.

What it takes to succeed has by this time been pretty well spelled out. The most important ingredient is an extremely visible presidential-level example. "Do as I do, folks, not just as I say." Other necessary pieces are the mounting of an intensive familiarization effort to ensure that all employees understand why improving the quality of products, production processes, and of the work environment is necessary and how it will positively affect their lives; the creation of a participative planning and problem-solving system to take advantage of total workforce expertise; the provision of adequate training in both technical and management systems areas; the implementation of some form of statistical quality control, where appropriate; the identification of a way to measure positive process results; and, finally, the organization of a system to coordinate and integrate all of the above.

A number of long-time professionals are capable of putting into place a model that includes all the necessary pieces. Most of these men work along with several associates and depend heavily on corporate resources and personnel. Most of them train on site, combining educational activities with actual on-going change efforts. Most of them begin producing positive results almost immediately but at the same time alert the client to the fact that it might take years to bring about the desired and necessary overall change. Most of them are relatively inexpensive. When a president with predominantly cultural skills wants to begin a quality improvement program and looks for professional assistance, these are the type of men to whom he or she turns.

The political president, however, has an entirely different perspective. He or she views a quality improvement effort mainly as an impression piece and is more interested in using it to enhance his or her image than in instigating actual change. The objective is to gain favorable publicity while keeping things tightly under control.

With the above in mind, the first thing that a political president usually does is to spend a lot of money. Because money is currently our major reward and is our standard for measuring success, the very fact that so much is being invested helps guarantee that people will take notice. After budgeting a million or so for the first year, the president goes out and buys a package deal that focuses on training rather than on action. Sizable numbers of employees are then sent away for several days, weeks, or months to an impressive, well-appointed facility where they struggle with the concept of quality, question their values and motives, and learn problem-solving skills.

The president does not usually take part in this training himself and soon turns project control over to a vice president, but with strict orders that no change in corporate policy, structure, or management style are to be made without his approval. At this point he has all that he needs and doesn't want to take any chances. He can tell his board and stockholders that the company has spent $2 million and trained 400 employees. He can speak publicly on quality and compare notes with other corporate presidents. He can even brag about the results of problem-solving group efforts and show how much money they have saved the company. At the same time, however, he has not forogtten his priorities and is not about to tolerate many of the adjustments we have identified as critical. For example, he has no intention of setting the example by delegating authority himself. While he might help force middle-level managers to involve hourly workers in operational decisions and problem-solving efforts, at least during the early stages of the exercise, he refuses to encourage or allow greater participation among his own direct reports. As we have indicated in Chapter 5, such an option is too threatening.

By way of summarizing Chapter 8, then, our traditional emphasis on image or appearances as opposed to content or performance is going to be difficult to overcome. It is reinforced by and in turn reinforces the other barriers to change that we have defined in previous chapters. It is also reinforced by our pride in the strides that modern man has made and by the increasingly powerful pen and brushstrokes of Madison Avenue.

Our best weapon in the battle to move on toward new world work, it seems, is the increasing awareness that despite the glamour, despite the on-going applause, image or appearances alone no longer suffice. The number of people like our friend Brian in Chapter 1 who have the feeling that they have succeeded without really succeeding is growing. There must, indeed, be more, and our determination to discover what that "more" might entail is mounting.

This, then, brings us to the last chapter in Part I and to our last concept, the concept of success. Success is that which is supposed to tie everything together into a meaningful whole. We know by now pretty much what success is not. In Chapter 9, therefore, we shall try to come up with a new, richer definition of what it is or of what it ought to be.

9

THE NEW FACE OF SUCCESS

In previous chapters we have discussed a number of roadblocks to our progress toward the development ethic and new world work, most of them quite serious. Modifying our current reality obviously is going to require radical shifts in both attitudes and values. The challenge involved is intensified by the fact that these individual roadblocks reinforce each other, thus creating a self-perpetuating system, a vicious cycle from which it will be extremely difficult to escape.

The reasoning behind the above observation goes like this. Because the conflict and political atmospheres, the machine-like repetitiveness, and the lack of challenge found in most corporate jobs makes the work itself unrewarding, the paycheck, as we have said, becomes the only payback that we can truly savor, the only motivation for doing what it is that we have been hired and trained to do. But outside the workplace while money, if properly used, can indeed facilitate our content-related efforts, its greatest short-term impact is in the world of image and appearances. One of the producers of this situation is the fact that we frequently can not find the time to invest along with our dollars that content-improving processes require. Too many of the necessary hours must be sacrificed in order to earn our paycheck.

The concept of time is obviously critical to our discussion. It will be dealt with more thoroughly in Chapter 10. Right now, however, all that I want to say is that the lack of necessary time reinforces our after-hours emphasis on gaining respect by buying and flaunting the right impression pieces, rather than on gaining it by demonstrating our ability to realize personal potentials.

In order to play the image game successfully, however, it is not only necessary to purchase the right impression pieces, as it was during my high school days, but contestants also must be able to afford things financially beyond the grasp of others. In order to afford things financially beyond the grasp of others—the Mercedes, the Dufour sailboats, the Bonanza airplanes, the Dunhill cigarette lighters—we obviously have to earn more money than they do, which brings us back to the beginning, for our major source of income is our job.

So round and round we go. The conflict mentality, the political atmosphere, and the lack of stimulation we encounter in the workplace make financial gain our only realistic objective. This reality pushes us toward the world of image on the outside. Our image fixation and the related need to be able to afford more expensive impression pieces than the competition on the outside, in turn, emphasizes money as the key to success and pushes us to fight for a larger salary and, as a result, toward conflict, politicization, and acceptance of an unstimulating environment on the inside.

The above realization is by no means new. For a long time now people have been seeking ways to break the cycle. Different schools of thought have chosen different points of attack in their efforts. Surveys, for example, have shown again and again that employees, if given a chance, want much more from their jobs than just money. After a certain level of financial security is reached, in fact, money frequently drops way down the list of priorities. One such survey was run by the magazine *Psychology Today*. An article in the May 1978 issue by Patricia Renwick and Edward Lawler entitled "What Do You Really Want From Your Job?" was based on input from 23,008 readers. Respondents were asked to rank both the importance of and their satisfaction with key job characteristics. In terms of importance, the top 12 were:

1. chances to do something that makes you feel good about yourself
2. chances to accomplish something worthwhile
3. chances to learn something new
4. opportunity to develop your skills and abilities

5. the amount of freedom you have on the job

6. chances you have to do the things you do best

7. the resources you have to do your job

8. the respect you receive from people with whom you work

9. amount of information you get about your job performance

10. your chances for taking part in making decisions

11. the amount of job security you have

12. the amount of pay you get

As we see, emphasis in the above results rests definitely on content and developmental issues rather than on gaining the increasing amounts of money necessary to our image battles.

From another direction we hear and read almost daily how unproductive it is to depend on our impression pieces for fulfillment and the respect we all covet. Groups like the 1960s' hippies and the Hari Krishnas have gone to extremes to prove to us how much better off we would be if we spent less time in the pursuit of money and more in the pursuit of inner peace. An increasing number of other, less radical proponents of a new lifestyle are espousing basically the same line. Obviously the cue cards and prompts are in place and are increasing in number. Still, however, very little new is happening on stage. The opinion expressed in the early part of this book, in fact, is that the audience is in for a long wait and that very little new will, indeed, materialize until some basic changes are made in our foundational definitions. The traditional definitions, the ones we persist in trying to build our performance on, though still quite solid, no longer fit our reality. They jam the machinery of our modern-day work world, keep the curtain from going up, and thereby thwart our efforts to succeed.

Part II of *Work and Rewards* has included a serious attempt to rework, or at least to help begin the reworking of, these foundational definitions. We have addressed the concepts of work, technology, rewards, and development. We have made a good start, but we are not yet finished, for just as the roadblocks discussed link together to create something much more insidious, much more difficult to deal with, our key definitions also must be linked together in order to generate a viable vision of the future, a vision of what success should and could be about once we have made the necessary commitment to change.

It has become obvious as we have proceeded that the change we are talking about has many parts. Each is necessary if we are to achieve our objective. At the same time, however, none of these parts individually or in partial groupings are sufficient in themselves to hatch our new version of success. They all must be incorporated into our efforts and coordinated if we are to prevail in our quest for the ultimate reward of respect.

This, then, is how I plan to end Part II. I am going to link all the new definitions that we have generated thus far into an expanded, modern-day definition of success, a definition that includes both what is *necessary* and what is *sufficient* in terms of what we wish to achieve. In essence, I am going to try to make a whole out of our efforts thus far so that we can get a glimpse of the overall challenge, so that we can begin developing some understanding of its magnitude and of its boundaries. Though this whole might at first seem a bit overwhelming and ponderous, putting it in perspective, in the long run, will make it easier to deal with. History has proven that definition is the most difficult part of problem solving. Once man is sure of what he is up against, once he is sure of the true nature of the problems faced, no matter how immense and multi-faceted, his tenacity tends to allow him to eventually discover and implement an appropriate solution.

So here it is, our enriched definition of success. Once it is in place we can move on to Section 3 and begin identifying the positive changes that should occur if society decides to transform itself, if it chooses to shift away from the outdated work ethic and toward a more appropriate, wholistic, and rewarding development ethic.

Success, according to our new definition, rests ultimately on the achievement of self-respect and societal respect once a decent level of wealth-based security is reached. I must emphasize, at this point, that I am talking about success and not envy. Envy differs greatly from success and is frequently the product of fourth-level accomplishments, of the creation of a role model solely through the accumulation of large amounts of money. Envy includes the desire to take something, in this case money, away from the "target," while respect is a noncombative emotion, one that focuses on reinforcing something positive in the person being complimented.

The people with the best chance of succeeding, of achieving self- and societal respect are those capable of first-, second-, and third-level accomplishments. They are the people on the first level who

make a large-scale contribution to society like inventing the computer or discovering a cure for cancer. They are the people on the
second level who make a smaller-scale contribution to a group with
which they are involved, like improving the quality of working life
for all secretarial-level staff in a corporation. They are the people on
the third level who don't make a direct contribution to any group
but provide a role model that encourages the development of others.

A prerequisite to all such accomplishments is the fullest possible
realization of our physical, intellectual, emotional, and spiritual
potential. Most of us are stronger in one of these areas than in the
rest. Balance, however, is again necessary if the best possible results
are to be achieved. When we focus too heavily on one facet of our
developmental efforts, the results can be counter-productive. For
example, we all know people who have concentrated almost exclusively on the development of their intellectual potential and, as a
result, are extremely awkward both physically and in their ability to
communicate their message effectively to others. Much of what they
have to offer, therefore, is lost, as well as a good part of the potential
payback in terms of respect. We all have also heard of or seen in
action top-level athletes whose temper tantrums attract more attention than their remarkable feats on the playing field. In such cases
the lack of emotional development gives a potentially positive role
model a black eye.

To continue, in order to fully realize the above defined physical,
intellectual, emotional, and spiritual potential we need access to the
inputs of plenty, truth, good, beauty, and power. Plenty generally
comes first and is the result of fourth-level accomplishments. Once
plenty is locked firmly into place, we are better able to concentrate
on our quest for truth, good, beauty, and power. Power relates to
our need for control, discussed in Chapter 2, and, therefore, is on a
slightly different plane from the others. Whereas plenty is not requisite to truth, especially in our information-saturated society, it is
supposedly not necessary to good, it is definitely not necessary to
beauty, and supposedly not necessary to power; whereas the same is
generally true for truth, good, and beauty in terms of the rest, it is
not true for power as we have defined it.

Without power over the sources of the other necessary developmental inputs, our continuing access to them is questionable at best.
The early Industrial Revolution proved that without some degree of
power over the sources of plenty, although we help generate large

amounts of wealth we will not necessarily be allowed to share in the division of the spoils. In terms of truth, the totally self-serving propaganda machines of dictatorships show that without some power over our society's sources of information we will not be able to gain access to what is desired. In terms of good, historical instances of its perversion and of the bending of those without power to the will of those in control are legion. Finally, those who desire beauty but enjoy no power over its source often end up with less than they had hoped for, if they end up with any at all.

In essence, then, while plenty is the gasoline that gets the engine started, power is the oil that makes the parts slide into place and work smoothly together.

All of the above folds neatly into what we call the development ethic. The development ethic is replacing the work ethic as the driving force in our society. In terms of our jobs, the development ethic says that our aim should be to spend as much of our time as possible in developmental and leisure work and as little as possible in slave, subsistance-level, and situation-improving efforts. The latter three are repetitious and require little thought once the process or technique involved is learned. They are built around the kinds of tasks that machines complete more efficiently than people. They contribute relatively little to the realization of our physical, intellectual, emotional, or spiritual potential when compared with developmental and leisure work.

With the above in mind, the developmental ethic goes on to say that modern technology, instead of being used to replace workers, should be used to free them from slave, subsistance-level, and situation improvement or sacrificial work so that they can invest their energies more fully in developmental and leisure, or new world efforts. This change alone will cause a major shift in our society's perspective. Instead of worrying about how to deal with the unemployed without bankrupting the economy or sparking violence, instead of our current welfare mentality, we will begin addressing the challenge of utilizing our society's potential more effectively in order to meet the constantly expanding range of opportunities generated in the developmental work marketplace.

The development ethic also moves us from a conflict orientation in the workplace to one that encourages teamwork. With teamwork as our major mode of interaction, political skills—or those which facilitate the manipulation of fellow employees on all levels in order to advance our own careers—will become less important, while technical and especially cultural skills will take center stage, cultural skills being those that provide the understanding of interpersonal, group, and social system/technical system interactions necessary for effective management.

Finally, the development ethic pushes us toward a better balance between our image and content orientation. It says that success does not so much involve the accumulation and flaunting of impression pieces provided by fourth-level accomplishments as it does gaining the desired respect through feats that demonstrate the realization of our physical, intellectual, emotional, and spiritual potential.

So there it is, our new world definition of success, the final, reworked foundational block. Perhaps we should think of this one as the keystone, the one that all the others support, but without which the others cannot stand. Whatever we decide to call it, however, now that it is in place we can begin rebuilding or reshaping our work lives and, in more general terms, our society, seeing what they will look like from our fresh, developmental perspective. With this objective in mind, then, let us move on to Part III of the book.

Part III

BROWSING AROUND
IN THE NEW WORLD

"To be what we are, and to become what we are capable of becoming, is the only end of life."

—Robert Louis Stevenson
Familiar Studies of Men and Books

10

REORIENTING THE
REALM OF PLENTY

An interview appeared in the January 16, 1984, issue of *U.S. News and World Report.* It was with James Baker, executive vice president of the General Electric Company. The title was "Industry Must Automate, Emigrate or Evaporate." Baker didn't say anything outlandish during the interview, anything that a lot of other top executives, academicians, consultants, and politicians aren't saying. In fact, at least during the first part he repeated what I have said in Chapter 4, that if we remain labor intensive we are going to lose, at least in the world market. Baker also agreed that the computer is possibly the first new technology that will not eventually create more jobs than it eliminates.

The latter part of the interview, however, was the part that I had trouble with, not necessarily because I disagreed with what he was saying, but because of its implications. The key question was whether or not jobs in the "new" industries resulting from automation and the computer revolution will pay as well as the "old" jobs being eliminated do. Baker thought not and cited evidence to support his conclusion, comparing wages earned in two new Silicon Valley firms with those earned in older industries in other parts of the country. It was his next answer, however, that really made me sit up. The result of this lower wage level, in Baker's opinion, will be that as things "progress" we will eventually see two parents or people in every family working in order to preserve the family's standard of living.

What he has given us here is a somewhat frightening contradiction. First of all, due to the nature of the new technology there won't be as many jobs. Second, because the jobs that remain will probably pay less, both parents will have to work in order to keep up. Less jobs, but more people working. How is that possible?

Even if both Baker and I are wrong and the new technology produces more instead of less jobs so that everyone can work, in our terms, at this point, he is no longer talking about situation-improving work. Rather, he is talking about a more sophisticated variety of subsistence-level work. What should add to our uneasiness is that if we, indeed, project present trends into the future, his conclusion about work seems valid. The growing pressures in the world marketplace, coupled with the increasing efficiency of computerized technology and with the mounting numbers of unemployed, will allow and force employers to pay less in order to stay competitive.

Baker's conclusions also bring another troubling question to mind. If in the near future there are enough jobs, but they don't pay as well, what will happen to the great number of families like Sharon's and Jakes's where both parents are already working in order to make ends meet, to enjoy life a little, and to put a little something away for old age? What must this type of family do in order to maintain its current standard of living?

Somehow, this doesn't sound like progress to me.

One of the issues already mentioned in Chapter 9 but not yet addressed in detail is that of time. We have talked about control, and time is obviously an important ingredient to control, but we have not made clear why. We can begin our effort to do so by making the obvious point that time is vital to every aspect of development. In order to fully realize our potential we require adequate wealth, adequate access to the necessary information, a fair shake, a soothing/stimulating environment, and adequate input into important decisions. But enough time, if we consider it, is just as important as any of the other prerequisites. Without time of our own we cannot make use of the available plenty, we cannot evaluate and shape the information at our disposal, we cannot take advantage of a fair shake and a supportive environment, and we cannot utilize our decision-making power. Without enough time of our own, then, the rest of the inputs necessary to development can be available but are of little or no value.

In terms of control over our time, some people are better off than others. Those in situation-improving, subsistance-level, and slave jobs don't usually enjoy as much as people holding developmental and leisure jobs. With this difference in mind our objective, as we have said, is to increase the amounts of developmental and leisure work in our lives. But according to Mr. Baker's predictions, our objective is not going to be reached. While the ideal is for technology to assist in our efforts to move in this direction, to "free" us, the reverse is apparently happening. The numbers are obvious. Dad has been working a 40-hour week. Because his new job doesn't pay as well, however, and because the old jobs are being automated, either dad now has to work 60 hours a week in order to maintain his family's quality of life, or mom has to take a part-time job and work 20 hours. As a family, then, we are now putting in 60 instead of 40 hours. We are, as a result, increasing the amount of time spent pursuing plenty and decreasing the amount spent pursuing the other required and desired inputs.

The effects of this backward progression, in my opinion, will be negative. For example, people are continually complaining about the deterioration of the family. They blame it on drugs, on various youth fads, on lack of discipline, on affluence. It is obvious to me, however, that one of the main culprits, if not *the* main culprit is, simply, the lack of time available for family activities. A family is a group of people related by blood or marriage who do and experience things together. If a majority of the members' waking hours, however, especially those of the parents, are consumed by responsibilities that do not allow the required contact, the family is going to suffer.

While parents frequently feel the effects of such deprivation more than we like to admit, it is obviously the children who are going to be the most severely victimized. Our younger tots will end up spending the best part of their active hours in day care centers, with relatives, or with babysitters. The older children, the adolescents and teenagers, will be increasingly on their own. All will receive less and less of the focused, personal, parental attention and patience so critical to development. At the same time, the parental attention they do receive will probably be less gratifying. Both mom and dad will now be tired when they get home from work. Both will have other things on their minds.

I have rarely met a healthy parent who did not want desperately to do the right thing by his or her children, who didn't regret not being able to give them what they need, both materially and emotionally. When grownups feel guilty about something, especially something that affects their kids, they try to make amends. In our projected future most of us won't be able to find more time to spend with Jane and Paul. Due to the shortage of jobs created by computer technology any attempt to do so might put us in the unemployment line, as it did Dustin Hoffman in the film "Kramer Versus Kramer." The most obvious way to compensate, therefore, will be by sharing our reward. We will try to make the kids feel that our absence during working hours was not a total loss. We will do so by offering them part of what we gained during those hours, and what we gained was money. In our efforts to make amends we will end up spending a good part of our salaries on gifts for our children, additional toys, unnecessary clothes, fancy cars, and expensive private schools. This frequently will be the only way we have of saying, "See, I really do care. I care a lot."

The consequence of such a gesture, however, no matter how sincere, can be unexpectedly negative. If a child is hungry enough for those things that only time and attention can provide—the touching, laughter, conversations and shared moments—if such shortages become a serious emotional issue, then gifts, through no one's fault, might eventually become confused with the real thing. Children might grow up viewing possessions as the key ingredient to happiness and contentment. On a societal scale, if this sort of substitution occurs frequently enough, our culture's image orientation and its focus on fourth-level accomplishments might actually intensify rather than ease into a more fruitful and satisfying balance with content and the other levels.

So what do we do? How do we reverse the negative trends alluded to by Mr. Baker and others? How do the plenty-generating institutions of the free enterprise system get back on track? The answer, of course, is found in our shift toward the development ethic. As this shift occurs, we will prove our above discussed projections wrong. The need of most individuals, in this context, is to find ways to generate more profits in less time, thus giving us increased access to both critical inputs.

In terms of increasing the amounts of profit available, the development ethic, for one thing, will encourage positive modifications in the way businesses are run. I have already discussed the new role technology will play. At the same time, a growing number of corporate leaders will realize that employees perform more effectively and produce better bottom line results when they are, indeed, team members, when they know that all those on the team are going to share both good times and bad, that all elements of the workforce, including top-level management, will receive more reward when the company prospers and less during periods of slack and readjustment. As a result of this realization, corporations will begin attempting more seriously to tie everyone's salary to the bottom line, using such vehicles as profit sharing and employee ownership to achieve their objective. Those with more power, due to their increasingly balanced perspective, will be less prone to use this power to take advantage of subordinates when the profits and losses are being divided up.

The above defined changes will, in turn, help blunt the negative impact of the three roadblocks to increasing the amounts of plenty generated—conflict, politicization, and our image orientation. In terms of conflict, those who spend a majority of their energies in defensive maneuvering, in protecting their turf, and in trying to discredit others will be less likely to succeed because the negative effects of their misguided energies on everyone's *financial* as well as emotional status will become more obvious. In terms of management skill sets, emphasis will shift away from the political and toward the technical and especially the cultural areas of expertise. Because companies will begin functioning more like teams and the "take" will be calculated on a team rather than on an individual basis, emphasis will be increasingly on understanding how the pieces should best fit together in order to maximize both short- and long-term results.

Finally, the steps described above will encourage the necessary swing toward performance and away from appearances as the major criterion for success. Those who have survived thus far by cultivating the appropriate image will have increasing difficulty in gaining the desired applause and support from their teammates. Employees will begin marking more closely exactly what their counterpart's contribution is to at least the financial betterment of the whole, and will be less reticent to protest when they see what they believe to be meaningless or detrimental activity.

In the final analysis, the fact that a well integrated team produces more plenty for the majority than does an aggregate of individuals pursuing their own selfish interests will become too obvious to ignore.

Employees will no longer feel that their main responsibility to the company is simply to put in the necessary number of hours, grab their paycheck, and run. Rather, they will feel that it is to become a useful part of a whole that has the objective of meeting everyone's needs fairly.

Now for the second issue, that of *time*. The question is, how do we free up more time for developmental and leisure work, for the kinds of work that allow us to realize our individual potential? Obviously the hours we are talking about must be taken away from the repetitious, machine-like subsistence-level and situation-improving types of work. But how do we accomplish this transition? And perhaps most important, how do we accomplish it without cutting both individual and corporate profits unacceptably, without undoing all the good done, in terms of increased profits, by adopting the team approach?

Before getting into this latter, more complex issue, let us address the mechanics of freeing up more time. Our first observation can be that, due to the "technology takeover" we are facing, the number of subsistence-level and situation-improving jobs found in factories, plants, and mills, those involving the *direct production of goods*, is gradually and in some cases not so gradually dropping off. At the same time, the number of subsistence-level and situation-improving staff and service sector jobs is reported to be growing. One of the things we know about staff employees, as well as a good percentage of employees in the service sector, is that they spend a majority of their working hours in an office. They do so for three reasons. The first and most frequently cited is that such sedentary "togetherness" facilitates communication, access to information, and corporate planning and problem-solving efforts. The second reason is that they do so in order to protect themselves by keeping close tabs on what is happening and by maintaining their network of supporters during office hours. The third reason is that this situation frequently allows bosses to maintain the desired level of control.

Some people also give a fourth reason. They say that our daily pilgrimage to the office fulfills our individual need for order and continuity. Based on the results of my informal study discussed in Chapter 4, however, I would disagree.

Offices as we know them today, in the opinion of a growing number of critics, are another bad habit. They are expensive in terms of both rent and maintenance. They swarm with distractions. It is becoming increasingly obvious that a majority of the people who push through the revolving door each morning could probably do what they come to do just as easily or more easily at home. For example, in terms of the desired communication, access to information, and the need for togetherness during planning and problem-solving efforts cited above, modern computer technology is capable of linking vocally, visually, or through instant printouts any number of employees sitting comfortably in their homes. In terms of the political problems mentioned, specifically the need to protect ourselves and the need to satisfy our bosses' desire for control, the team approach will make the necessary difference. First, because teams understand the value of every member's contribution, teammates will be more likely to protect each other than to pounce. Second, because our bosses will begin to function more as coordinators and facilitators than as warlords, control will become less of an issue. Emphasis will be on supporting rather than on dominating or defeating.

One relatively obvious way of freeing more time, then, is by using computer technology and the team approach to reduce the number of hours necessarily spent doing subsistence-level, situation-improving, and developmental work in the office, to create more telecommuters, not just on the secretarial and sales level, but on all levels.

For example, I recently talked with a rather downcast young director. When I asked what was wrong, he told me the following story. His division had not been functioning smoothly or doing a good job. The division vice president had finally called all his direct reports together and announced that things had to change, and that he was holding each of them responsible for figuring out ways to make their units more productive. He encouraged them to think creatively, to question their normal way of meeting responsibilities, and to come up with more effective alternatives.

My friend had taken the challenge seriously. He had immediately called his staff together to begin examining their work habits. As it turned out, most of his people were involved in projects at production facilities rather than at corporate headquarters where their offices were located. Mondays were spent in staff meetings reviewing what had happened during the previous week and planning the new week's activities. On Tuesdays his staff started traveling. The rest of the week was frequently spent either at a project site or writing reports. If people stayed out until Friday, their reports were written in a motel room. The telephone put them in touch with any necessary corporate information source. When they got back they went straight home, frequently late Friday night or on Saturday morning. If people were finished with their field work by Thursday or early Friday morning, however, they were required to return to the office.

The staff realized that this latter requirement was a bad habit and largely a waste of time. Anything they did during those few, tired hours in the office could be done just as easily and much more comfortably at home while seated at the kitchen table or in their study. This train of thought had led to discussions of the wear and tear of so much travel, of the constant tiredness, and of the resentment felt at having so little time to spend with families. During the conversation, the director learned that all those involved lived in the same general area outside the city and suggested that they begin holding their Monday morning sessions at his home. Afterward, if people had other meetings scheduled they could come individually into the city office.

As a result of these changes, the department's morale picked up noticeably, as did its performance. Reports started coming in from the operational side of the business about the good job his departmental staff was doing, although members were now actually spending fewer hours than before working, or working and commuting. The director had been extremely pleased with himself, and when the vice president asked him to come to his office one day, he had assumed that it would be for congratulations. After some small talk, the vice president had asked about the changes in his staff's routine. When the director explained the decisions that his people had made and the reasoning behind them, however, he had not received the expected response. Instead, the vice president had frowned and shook his head. "It won't work, Mat. You're setting a bad example. I'm beginning to hear a lot of grumbling. People walk past your empty, dark offices and wonder what's going on. They wonder why they should continue coming in when your group doesn't seem to feel the need to."

The director had defended his position, recalling the original charge and pointing to the positive results achieved by doing what he had been told to do. Later on in the conversation he had finally suggested that, rather than concentrating on forcing his group to return to its old habits, the others should perhaps also begin looking for ways to free up more of their own time. The vice president had not agreed.

Despite the outcome, this director had obviously been on the right track in terms of what we consider important.

A second way to free more time is through the various forms of job sharing. In job sharing, two or more employees take turns filling the same position or positions. But while only one at a time is performing the required tasks, he or she has continual access to the expertise of the other members. Successful job sharing, of course, presumes the existence of a cooperative rather than a conflict relationship. It is currently being practiced in a variety of forms in a wide range of businesses, but it is not yet what I would consider a trend and will not gain popular acceptance until the cultural changes that we have discussed take place.

Both of the above possibilities offer us control over increasing amounts of our time. Both, however, obviously cost something in terms of the bottom line, which brings us back to the issue of how we can increase the amount of time not spent under the control of someone else while simultaneously maintaining an adequate level of income, an adequate intake of plenty. In order to work at home, for example, we need at least a computer and a telephone. If we have 2,000 people working at home, this can add up. How are we going to pay these costs? Part of the answer, of course, as we have said, is that we will not be paying rent on as much space, and we will not be paying as much for maintenance. It is obvious that the savings involved will defray at least part of the new expense. In terms of job sharing, a second alternative we have discussed, the outlay for team salaries, at first glance, will probably exceed the income produced. One job will have to support two or even three people, or two jobs will support three people. If we take a longer-term perspective, however, the imbalance involved diminishes. For one thing, again as we have said, the person currently in control will be more effective because he or she will have a greater pool of expertise from which to draw. At the same time, the off-duty person might be studying a new technology or management system that will enhance team performance. A second off-duty person might be helping organize a community drug education program for high school students, thus helping to improve the corporation's image and sales.

It seems that the answer to this issue has several parts. The above are some of the micro solutions possible. On the macro level, let us talk about ways in which the development ethic will affect the *distribution* as well as the *generation* of profits. Because money will no longer be the only reward sought in the "new world," and because of the pervading team mentality, there will be more of a willingness to close the salary gap. No one will really need to make more than, say, $200,000 a year in order to meet his or her developmental needs. Anything more than that will be classified, and rightly so, as an impression piece and will fail to arouse the envy and admiration that it does today. In terms of the alternative of job sharing, team members on most middle- and upper-range pay levels will probably be willing to trade at least part of any further salary increase for the additional free time gained.

Another part of the macro answer, related to and facilitating the above, has to do with inflation. People often demand more salary than they need in order to build what they believe to be an adequate nest egg. They do so as a hedge against inflation. "Inflation," according to the dictionary, is an "abnormal increase in available credit and currency beyond the proportion of available goods." This "abnormal increase" causes prices to go up. A victim's definition might be that inflation occurs when, no matter what we do, we can't seem to get ahead. We work harder, we work longer hours, we learn new skills, we go to the bargaining table, we strike in order to increase our salary. We hope this larger salary will allow us to purchase more of the required and desired goods and services. But, at the same time, the price of the goods and services we require and desire continues to rise, so that our efforts are for naught. I once helped with a project at a paper mill in a small, northern Louisiana town. The mill was the largest employer in the area. The town's economy depended largely on it. As a result of this situation, every cost-of-living or negotiated salary increase received by employees was automatically followed or even preceded by a rise in prices at the local stores, allowing the employees to simply keep up rather than to improve their quality of life. That's inflation.

Controlling inflation is obviously a key objective of any economic system. Inflation can be dangerous. It can cause crippling balance of payment problems. It can bring down governments. It can help produce situations that lead to war. A tremendous amount of energy historically has been invested by the world's leaders in attempts to discover ways to control inflation. One traditional way of doing this is by raising interest rates. As a result of such raises people and organizations are less willing to live on credit. Because fewer people are depending on credit and, therefore, less money is available in the marketplace, the competition between sellers becomes more intense.

Profit margins are cut. Sellers are less willing to risk a loss of business by seeking greater gain.

Inflation, however, according to every economist that I have read, is endemic to free enterprise. It will never be totally eliminated. There will always be some inflation in our system. It cannot, therefore, be solely the result of abnormal increases in available currency and credit. In my opinion, in fact, there is nothing at all abnormal about what happens. Rather, inflation results from everyone's very normal desire to get ahead once a reasonable level of wealth-based security has been reached. Quite simply, we want to spend more money than frequently we earn in order to buy those things that we think are important. The thought is, "If I could just squeeze a few more bucks out, a few hundred or thousand more out, I could afford that club membership, that cycle, or that boat." Inflation in our system, therefore, is a natural product of the things we discussed in Part I.

When we shift to the development ethic, however, I believe that inflation will be more easily controlled. Inflation is not, by definition, endemic to the free enterprise system. Rather, in my opinion, it is endemic to free enterprise systems in situations where increased plenty is the sole or dominant objective. When we shift to the development ethic our resultant perspective will become more holistic. Money, as we have said, will be demoted. Rather than an end in itself, it will become increasingly a means for facilitating the acquisition of other inputs valuable to the realization of our potential. Because most of these other inputs will cost less than impression pieces, getting ahead and gaining the desired respect will no longer necessitate spending more than the other guy, and it will no longer necessitate borrowing as much as possible. The amount of credit and currency flowing into the marketplace, therefore, will probably remain in better balance with the proportion of goods available.

In terms of society as a whole, I believe that acceptance of the development ethic will help us deal more successfully with yet another serious problem resulting from our current over-emphasis on the acquisition of plenty. That problem is poverty. We obviously possess the resources and talent needed to eradicate poverty in the United States. We obviously feel the need to help those with little or no chance of leading a decent life, much less of realizing their potential. The major obstacle, then, is not lack of resources or desire.

Rather, I believe it is our approach to the problem. Due to our traditional fixation on increased plenty as the best all-around solution, we continue to base a majority of our efforts to eradicate poverty on the misguided belief that the most critical ingredient to improving one's situation is money. At the same time, however, we do not want to *give* the needy too much of this critical input. First, we do not want to for fear of killing incentive. Second, we do not want to because we do not believe that they should be given a free ride when the rest of us have worked so hard and sacrificed so much to get where we are. With the work ethic guiding our thoughts, these arguments are legitimate. As a result, we give the needy just barely enough to survive on and expect them to do the rest. Our actions, however, show ignorance of the fact that if the needy had possessed the skills necessary to "dig themselves out" in the first place, they would not have chosen to fall into or to remain buried in the pit of poverty.

Another related weakness of this approach is that, due to the "every man for himself" attitude encouraged by the free enterprise system when money is our major or only reward, the poor, due to their vulnerability, frequently become targets for the less scrupulous. We give money to the poor in the form of welfare, child support, and so on because we want them to learn how to handle it and, in so doing, to feed it back into the system. In actuality, they do feed it back or have it taken back, but not always in a way that improves their situation. Anyone who has spent time asking questions or visiting stores or housing facilities in a poor neighborhood understands the truth of this statement. High prices for low-quality goods and services, apparently liberal credit terms that turn out to be a trap, and exorbitant rents for poorly-maintained apartments are a normal part of life. In many ways, then, trying to help the poor by simply giving them money can make their situation worse instead of better.

If we view poverty from the perspective of the development ethic, however, our approach becomes more comprehensive. The question we must ask from this perspective is, "What does it take to allow the poor, or at least their children, to realize their physical, intellectual, emotional, and spiritual potential so that they also can eventually contribute to society's development?" The answer we get is not that different, we discover, from the answer that we have derived for ourselves, except perhaps in terms of priorities and in terms of the means of provision. In essence, it takes emphasis away from money-based benefits as the major remedy and puts it on the provision of adequate educational opportunity, adequate legal assistance, a decent living environment, and, finally, the chance to increase individual control over individual destiny in our on-going quest for respect.

In summary, then, we see that our quest for plenty will take on a different meaning in the free enterprise system if we adapt it to the development ethic. It will gradually lose its dominance and fall into a more productive role. It will more readily facilitate societal and individual progress while generating fewer unnecessary hurdles. Ultimately, it will make our lives more challenging, fuller, and more imaginative. It will help us, truly, to progress into a new era and to create a new, healthier living environment.

11

EDUCATION MOVES
TO THE FRONT ROW

If the corporate sector is successfully to set the example in terms of our move toward the new world, it must address two critical issues related to our education system. The first is, "How can and should this system prepare future managers to encourage and practice the things we have been discussing, such as teamwork and the loosening of bounds on information important to individual development?" Traditionally, it has provided business majors with a set of relevant technical skills and provided them with a feeling for what is needed in order to "fit." But what should our educational system offer in the new world? The second, more general question that relates to society as a whole is, "How should our educational institutions be reorganized so that they might play a more positive role in a society dedicated to the new ethic?" Obviously, when we increasingly make overall development our primary objective and the traditional, relatively isolated quest for plenty less so, some fairly radical changes will occur. What will the nature of these changes be?

In order to address the first question, I sent for the 1988–89 Masters in Business Administration program bulletin from the Wharton School and the 1987–88 MBA bulletin from the Harvard Business School. The purpose of an MBA is to give students the skills to run businesses, or to train managers. As we have said, the employees of any successful business possess two critical sets of positive

skills. These are technical skills and cultural skills. Technical skills—
engineering, accounting, financial, marketing, human resource, and
so on—are most important at the specialist level. Future managers,
one might assume, are employees with proven technical skills who
have also shown an aptitude for leadership and have demonstrated
the ability to understand how the organization works. With this in
mind, one might also assume that the purpose of the MBA degree
program is to improve the cultural, or leadership and systems skills
of such rising stars. This, however, is not generally the case.

Originally, MBA programs catered mainly to students fresh from
their undergraduate training. Because a large percentage of these had
not majored in business, or because even those who had majored in
business were suspect in their ability to address adequately the technical challenges of the corporate world, or because there was really
nothing else to do since the cultural realm was not yet a serious consideration, MBA programs focused again on technical skills. A vast
majority of them still do, although most of our current MBA students are now full-time employees, rather than being fresh out of college.

The Wharton program, for example, according to the *Graduate
Division MBA Course Guide 1988–89*, requires a management core
of eight course units, one business policy unit, five major units, and
five elective units. Of the eight management core units, seven are
quantitative, or technically oriented. These include Accounting,
Microeconomics, Macroeconomics, Financial Analysis, Marketing,
Quantitative Methods, and Statistical Analysis for Managers. Only
the Management of People at Work addresses cultural issues. Almost
all of the five unit majors—Accounting, Decision Sciences, Finance,
Insurance and Actuarial Science, Marketing, Public Policy and Management, Real Estate, Transportation, Arts Management, Legal
Studies, and Statistics—again focus on technical skills and issues.
Only one—Management—specifically focuses on what we consider to
be cultural issues.

Where, then, do our managers of the future learn the necessary
cultural skills? Two other alternatives exist. The first is through
actual on-the-job experience. The second is as a result of in-house
training, of that provided by the corporation. When evaluating the
potential of the first alternative, we run head-on into the conflict
mentality. The presumption of superiors, frequently correct, is that,
"My underlings will push me aside and take my place at the first

opportunity. Their objective is to steal my job. Therefore, I must be careful about what I allow. Play up their technical skills, the results of which will also make me look good. Play down their cultural skills, for that's where the threat lies."

I have known a number of companies where the above mind-set was in evidence and, as a result, ended up being forced to bring in "new blood" when management-level positions opened up. The rationalization for this move was that new people brought along new ideas and helped keep the perspective fresh. The truth of the matter was usually that bosses had intentionally kept their subordinates "dumb," and that subordinates had played dumb in order to survive, so that when managerial positions came open the boss was forced to say, "No one here."

A second tendency of those who don't really want to take the chance of training potential competitors is to bring in ex-military personnel. I frequently have been surprised by the number of retired officers filling high-level corporate positions. Some of them, of course, have made the effort to learn what they needed to learn and have adjusted well to their new roles. I suspect, however, that many others have been hired mainly because someone believed that they already possessed all the characteristics necessary for a good manager. First, they knew how to obey orders with a minimum of questions. Second, they had been trained to be loyal to their "commanders."

For corporate politicians whose major concern is staving off attacks, these characteristics are extremely attractive. Politicians need direct subordinates willing to function like cogs in a well-oiled machine; they need subordinates whose loyalty is proven and who are good implementers rather than question askers and challengers. Soldiers fill this bill. The strengths inculcated into them during their military careers are right on target. Unfortunately, these same strengths all too often conflict with the reality of the business world and function as a handicap in an environment much more turbulent and demanding than that previously experienced, an environment where uncertainty is the norm and where the ability to ask the right questions is frequently much more important than the ability to take orders.

Concerning in-house training, most sizable corporations have such programs. They are run by a director of training who reports to the vice president of human resources. Training directors are responsible for organizing and overseeing performance evaluations, career path charting, and the training necessary to advancement. The people who provide that training are in-house experts, consultants from firms specializing in various areas, or academia-based consultants. I have laying before me several training manuals from Johnson and Johnson (J&J), a corporation considered by many to be one of the country's most progressive. These manuals, indeed, focus on at least one aspect of the cultural dimension. They stress such things as the development of judgement, maturity, leadership, innovativeness, of a risk-taking mentality, of common sense and self-motivation, of the ability to communicate, of image, and of an appropriate value system. The objective of the J&J training program is to enhance important individual strengths and to develop interpersonal skills. Well-designed in-house courses are offered in the above areas, or candidates are sent to external training facilities set up by consulting firms.

The input into the J&J management training effort, as well as into the training efforts of every other progressive corporation with which I am familiar, are well thought out, well organized, and useful. They are not, however, *complete*, according to our concept of what training in cultural skills should include. Cultural skills grow from the two types of understanding briefly defined in Chapter 5. The first, which is generally well-covered by corporate training programs, is the understanding of what it takes to be a good leader and member of a team. The second, however, which I consider to be of equal importance and which is not at all well-covered by corporate training programs, is an understanding of how organizations work and how they should work, of how the various parts fit together to make up a whole, of how that whole fits into the larger whole of which it is a part, of how the whole is different from the parts it includes, of what the "glue"— the systems of communications, production, information, incentives, command, problem solving, and planning—is that binds this whole together.

What we are talking about in terms of this second area of knowledge is the development of an appropriate "systems" perspective to complement the future manager's leadership and team-building skills. The difference between these two sides of the cultural skills coin can be made clearer by this example. The manager possessing interpersonal and team-building but not systems skills, when faced with a problem such as falling productivity, traces it to the individual or employee group involved, tries to discover its roots, then attempts to remedy it by altering individual or group behavior. The person possessing systems skills as well suspects that the same problem might stem from the way the work, reward, communication, information, or perhaps problem-solving systems involved are organized and often begins his or her probe by looking at systemic interfaces, moving from there to the individuals involved, if necessary.

In terms of systems training, the Harvard Business School MBA Program 1988 Bulletin shows at least an understanding of the need for it. The bulletin lists as a program goal preparation of its "students to assume general management responsibilities." It calls for the development of a "generalist perspective," for development of the ability to view the "entirety of an organization as well as its place in a larger environment." The bulletin's presentation then proceeds, however, to revert to the norm, focusing, in terms of course requirements, on technical specializations. It requires students to become more familiar with the traditional cross-section of them: Control, Finance, Human Resources Management, Marketing, and Production and Operations Management. It also requires courses more general in nature: Management Communication; Managerial Economics; Organizational Behavior; Business, Government, and the International Economy; Managing Information Systems; and Competition and Strategy. These courses, however, are still relatively technical-skill-specific. What is missing in the above are the courses that tie all these individual parts together and show how they should interact in order to make up a successful whole. Only the one second-year requirement, Management Policy and Practice and the Management Simulation Exercise, begin to address this critical task.

Generally speaking, then, neither in-house training nor that received from academia successfully delivers the second segment of knowledge critical to the generation of well-rounded cultural skills, the systems segment. Until this situation is corrected, it can be fairly well guaranteed that we will continue to encounter management problems at all levels; that we will continue to run into supervisors, directors, and vice presidents who don't really seem to have a grasp of the total picture; and that we will continue, as a result of this lack of appropriate perspective, to move into projects without paying adequate attention to their long-term consequences.

It can also be fairly well guaranteed that we will be forced to continue wondering why the politicians go on winning when so many others obviously possess superior talent and potential, although the answer to this second puzzle should be fairly apparent by now. It is this: Basically, as one progresses upward through the ranks of management, the systems portion of critical understanding and skills becomes increasingly important. When such understanding and skills are lacking, when they have not been gained either from in-house or academic training sessions, and when technical skills no longer suffice to deal with the complex, multidisciplinary problems that are upper-level management's lot, a great number of managers are forced to rely increasingly on political skills to survive. Unfortunately, the interpersonal and leadership skills necessary to complement systems skills also complement political skills, thus helping to make the politician more effective in his or her endeavors.

As we begin moving toward the development ethic, however, all this should change. Because the job's main benefit will be the realization of one's overall potential, our focus will expand. In an effort to define what colleges and universities should offer in the future, a group including the now-retired board chairman of Air Products and Chemicals; the president and CEO of Bethlehem Steel; the president and CEO of Mack Truck; a vice president with AT&T; a retired president, CEO, and board chairman of the International Paper Company; a vice president of finance with the Greif Companies; the president, CEO, and Board Chairman of the Fuller Company; the CEO and board chairman of the First Valley Bank; and myself put together a model of what we believe the college and graduate management training curriculum should be. Future business majors, first of all, should receive a broad, liberal arts background to give them a holistic perspective concerning life in general. The undergraduate business major itself should include introductory courses in the key areas of specialization—production, finance, accounting, marketing, and human resources management—in order to give students an overview, a general framework into which they can fit their future decisions and training. One or two courses beyond the introductory level course in the chosen area of technical expertise should suffice to prepare students for any entry-level position in the business world. This opinion is based on the group's unanimous agreement that most of any employee's relevant technical skills, with the possible exception of the typist's and the computer programmer's, are learned on the job, no matter how much previous training has been received.

Upon graduating, students should take a job rather than move directly into an MBA program. They should do so in order to gain the practical experience that brings theory to life, that encourages them to pay more attention to what is being taught than to grades. As I have said before, I have taught MBA students, both those who are working and those fresh out of college. There is no comparison. The younger set is almost totally grade oriented. Due to their lack of experiential credentials, grades are critical in terms of impressing recruiters. They are involved in a game, but a deadly serious one with As rather than business-related expertise as the prize. It is somewhat like teaching an athlete to play quarterback when he or she has never played football. Such students learn the moves but never achieve a feel for their real situational value. In such classes the teacher has to provide the questions as well as the answers.

Working MBAs, however, already know most of the questions. They know what the problems are and come looking for answers. They have a pretty good idea of what they need to accomplish in order to improve their job situation, and it has little to do with whether an A+ or a B– is earned. The MBA itself is considered necessary to their advancement, but emphasis in class rests on learning something of value.

Again, this point was unanimously agreed upon by the group. It also agreed, however, that formal education should not stop entirely between the undergraduate and MBA levels. Rather, a group of courses to improve technical skills should be offered, with on-the-job and in-house training complementing formal classes. Employees should be able to take such courses in more than one area of technical expertise if they wish to move around in the company; and such moving around will become more common because, first, it will obviously be advantageous to the company and, second, when our focus shifts from beating our co-workers to learning from them, the desire to move will increase so that we can gain access to a greater variety of inputs.

Finally, students should not be eligible to enroll for MBA training until they have received at least two recommendations from bosses. This latter requirement will help encourage potential managers to deal with at least their technical shortcomings beforehand, rather than after the fact.

As a result of these changes, MBA programs will be able to focus more on the cultural dimension. One cluster of core courses will address leadership, group process, and team-building skills. A second cluster will concentrate on generating the necessary systems perspective. Finally, a third cluster will focus on the corporation's relationship with the larger system of which it is a part—the marketplace, the community, the environment, the nation, and world. One specific thing that this curriculum adjustment will accomplish will be to help shift us away from our current managerial fixation with numbers that was discussed in Chapter 7. In terms of our move toward the development ethic, another major benefit will be that this shift will bring the business and academic communities closer together. For one thing, obviously there will be more emphasis on research and development (R&D). Due to our culture's current over-emphasis on the generation of plenty, on bottom line, and short-term results, often at the expense of longer-term perspective and success, R&D frequently gets short-changed. It is treated as somewhat of a luxury and is the first thing to go when times get hard and dollars tight. This is another bad habit, the false logic of which should be obvious. R&D is becoming possibly *the* most critical factor in many industries as our level of technical and product innovation continues to accelerate.

With the development ethic's modified attitude toward the importance of the bottom line, with its increased emphasis on developmental work and on giving employees more creative challenges to meet while computers take care of the "grunt" work, R&D will be given the status and attention it deserves. The value of collaboration between the industrial and academic sectors on R&D projects will also become increasingly obvious. Relations between these two sectors are currently strained, especially on the management as opposed to technical problem-solving side. Managers frequently think that academicians are arrogant, unrealistic, aloof, and impractical in what they propose or demand. Academicians, in turn, frequently consider managers and executives to be ignorant, stubborn, ungrateful, and paranoid in their resistance to anything new, no matter how obvious the benefits. I don't believe that I have ever talked with a Ph.D. in a university business department who hasn't eventually voiced frustration over the inability or reluctance of managers to comprehend, much less to implement, relatively simple changes proven to have a positive effect on the bottom line as well as on the working environment.

The management side of the issue is well presented, I think, by this passage taken from a letter that I received from a retired president/CEO of the Gould Corporation.

Years ago at Gould we had nineteen Ph.D.s on the payroll. Only one was in a management position. He did his best to convince management and the Board that this group could be developed into useful general employees instead of being placed on duties calling for "specialized or tunnel vision." The few cases that were tried, however, all ended in disaster since the members of the group always felt that their answers and reports were infallible and not to be discussed or questioned by those who did not have their I.Q. or training.

The core problem here seems fairly simple. Most of those with a great deal of academic training who interact with corporations are selling either technical or cultural skills. At the same time, most of the problems faced by modern companies in this country, be they technical or cultural, are viewed by managers as having a critical political component that must be dealt with first before anything else can be accomplished. What we run into, then, is a perception barrier. The two groups—the theory-oriented Ph.Ds and the real world-oriented managers—are frequently talking about two different things, speaking, as it were, two different dialects, although they use basically the same words. The overlap is sometimes hard to define.

In this regard, several important things will happen when we shift to the development ethic. First, when emphasis in the corporate world moves from the political dimension toward the technical and cultural dimensions, the services offered by the highly educated will become more meaningful. Second, scholars will be more eager to climb down from the security of their ivory towers in order to broaden their perspective, to enhance their own development, and to mix it up. More and more of those trained as teachers will opt to spend time in industry. At the same time, more and more of those trained as managers will opt to teach in order to gain access to a greater variety of developmental inputs. In terms of job sharing, for example, the various members of the team will spend a larger part of their careers in academia, first as students and later, perhaps, as teachers.

Now it is time to address our second critical question, "How should our educational institution be reorganized to play a positive role in a society dedicated to the new world development ethic?"

First of all, in order to meet the greater variety of demands placed on it by such a transition, it will have to become increasingly flexible and efficient. A major modern-day complaint concerning the public school system, at least, is that the number of administrators seems to be increasing more rapidly than the number of teachers. This situation is a never-failing indicator of growing inflexibility and inefficiency. A comparable situation in the business world is the company where the number of managers is growing more rapidly than the number of direct producers. Corporate leaders are currently trying to correct this imbalance by collapsing their levels of management. In the public education system, however, the bottom line incentive to such change is missing. Survival is not dependent on the efficiency of the operation. When I was young and idealistic I thought that our country should do away with private schools and force wealthy kids into the public system so that their parents would begin contributing to the solution of its problems. Now that I am older and a little more pragmatic, I believe that we should, instead, do away with the public school system as we know it because, while continuing to drain our budgets, it is not producing the desired results and will remain incapable of doing so until radical change occurs.

One of these changes should be the creation of some sort of bottom line by which to judge performance. An approach to this challenge already being tried is the voucher system. According to this system, quite simply, the government gives students funds in the form of vouchers with which to pay for their education. In turn, the students are allowed to cash these vouchers in at any public school that they choose. The schools, as a result of the arrangement, are now forced to compete for "customers." Student bodies are no longer guaranteed. When a school continues to deliver poor-quality education, it is eventually forced out of business. Schools that maintain and enhance the calibre of their product, however, attract increasing numbers of students and generate growing amounts of "profit." This profit can be used to expand operations, to increase salaries, to pay bonuses, or to invest in technology that will further facilitate delivery.

Our current failure to use technology as effectively as possible in education is a second critical issue as important as and resulting at least in part from the lack of a bottom line. An interesting point made by Lewis J. Perelman in his article, "The Future of Learning: The Age of School Is Over," that appeared in the March 30, 1986, issue of *The Orange County Register* was that classroom instruction is the only one out of nearly 20 "communication media" identified by a 1983 Massachusetts Institute of Technology study with falling productivity during the preceding 20 years. This drop was credited at least partially to an unwillingness to take advantage of modern technology.

If we switch to the development ethic and begin to think of technology as something with the ability to free us for more interesting work, rather than as something created to replace teachers in this instance, this attitude should change. The incorporation of mechanical aids into our plans will not only make teachers more productive in terms of delivery, but will make the entire system more cost effective. Increased amounts of higher-quality information will be deliverable at lower cost.

Appropriate use of technology, at the same time, will change the role of the teacher. With video screens, computers, television, and so on delivering most of the required data and doing a good part of the testing, teachers will be able to spend more of their time facilitating the educational process, encouraging students to learn how to learn, and enhancing the desire to learn. The teachers from whom I believe I learned the most—Ms. Merwin, Ms. Mahoney, Ms. Widner, Ms. Miller, Mr. Dan Helwig, and "Doc" Wible—were not necessarily the ones who demonstrated the best understanding of their subject. Rather, they were the teachers who took a personal interest in me as a student, who treated me as a unique individual with promise of some sort. Emphasis, I suspect, will be on producing more teachers like these. Psychological and interpersonal skills will become more important than presentation skills. Teacher training will focus increasingly on providing the tools and techniques that facilitate the realization of student potential, and decreasingly on providing those that facilitate the generation and distribution of information.

A current example of this "new breed" is a young high school English teacher named Ray Oswald. A while ago Ray shared his concern with me about a portion of his classes that "wouldn't try." These students did just enough work to pass, or not enough, or none at all. Their explanation was that what he taught had no real bearing on their lives. Most of these kids worked on farms or already had part-time, low-level jobs and expressed no desire to go on to college. Ray, however, was convinced that if he could find a way to get them involved, they would end up profiting. The major constraint, of course, was time. How does a teacher find the time necessary to deal with issues like these without short-changing other responsibilities?

Ray's eventual solution was to announce that no one would be allowed to fail his course, that students would be required to retake tests until they showed an acceptable understanding of the subject matter, and that after each test he would spend whatever extra time necessary going over the points missed. In terms of our discussion, Ray had turned, with this group at least, to exploring the limits of their potential. He had, in effect, switched from the traditional ranking perspective to a developmental one. The price he paid for this decision was the additional hours dedicated to his new responsibilities. If educational systems made better use of technology, however, more decisions like Ray's probably would be possible.

The issue of ranking will obviously also take on a new light when we adopt the development ethic. School is currently another battlefield where the conflict is frequently just as fierce as it is in the corporate world. We wondered earlier why, if on the playing field we become so embued with the team spirit, it does not carry on into the world of work? Part of the answer, I think, is that while a good portion of our youth is, indeed, spent on the playing field, a larger portion is spent in the classroom, and here the reward system normally pits us against one another. Emphasis is on seeing who is going to beat whom, on seeing who is going to get the A, who will get into the good college, into the good graduate school. Test scores are paramount, and test scores are earned through individual and not team effort. One's ability or potential ability to coordinate activities with others is largely or totally ignored in the classroom when defining success. This attitude, then, is the one we normally carry on into the world of work. It eclipses our team orientation gained on the playing field.

With adoption of the development ethic, our most important rewards, as we have said, will become qualitative rather than quantitative in nature. Because quantitative rewards are limited, while qualitative rewards are not, the need to fight it out, to beat someone out of something, will subside. Our focus in academia, therefore, instead of being on streamlining our method for picking the winner, will shift increasingly toward improving ways to encourage the enhancement of everyone's understanding so that students can enjoy their potential and contribute more fully. At the same time, due at least partially to our new attitude, access to high-quality education will become more a given and less a privilege gained by earning higher grades or having more money. Every classroom from the Sesame Street set on up, through technology, will be able to offer well-orchestrated presentations and lectures by top people in a wide variety of fields and will be able to offer it in an entertaining and cost-effective manner.

Finally, from the teacher's viewpoint this time, a current, serious complaint is parental apathy, or the lack of parental interest in their children's education. According to Marguerite Michael's article, "A Report Card From Our Teachers," in the December 1, 1985, issue of *Parade* magazine, mom and dad are "too permissive," "not at home," "not creating an environment at home conducive to learning." Based on our observations in previous chapters, the "not at home" comment is the critical one. It's hard to pay adequate attention to our children's education and to create a proper environment when both mother and father spend 8 to 10 hours a day in activities that require their being somewhere else. Time, again, is the critical element, and when we shift to the development ethic emphasis, as we have said, will be on giving people increased control over their time. One of the results of the interaction between this increased control and our more appropriate use of communications technologies should be that parents will, indeed, begin playing a larger and more direct role in the education of their children. The home will increasingly become a learning center that should eventually rival even the school, at least in terms of the amount of information we can access and the amount of focused, quality attention the individual student can receive.

In summary, then, when we adopt the new ethic, reorient our value system, use technology to free people for more of their own and their children's/student's developmental pursuits, and begin focusing more on the content of our lives than on the image we present, our situation in terms of "truth" should improve. Education and teaching will move to the front row where they belong and gain the respect that they merit. Rather than remaining servants to a 19th century industrial society, rather than continuing to focus on grinding out human machine parts, our educational institutions will become an equal partner to our economic ones in a relationship appreciated and profited from by all.

12

GOOD AS GOOD CAN BE

It is obvious that when we begin talking about encouraging the dissemination of "good" in the workplace, about honoring the employees' desire for assurances that a fair deal will be received, that they will be given credit when credit is due and will not be victimized by those with more power, we are talking about important attitudinal and behavior changes. When we discuss the realization, cited in Chapter 2, that the satisfaction of employee needs, including that for good, is more important to the success of the company as well as the individual than the satisfaction of the needs of any other group with a stake in the operation, the value of these changes becomes increasingly obvious. In previous chapters we have discussed at length the nature of the factors currently hampering our efforts to institute them. There is one more factor, however, or perhaps I should say "confusion" impeding our progress that must be talked about because it remains a major obstacle, especially to the enhancement of our opportunity to obtain good, as defined, in the workplace.

This factor is more "nuts and bolts" than the rest. At the same time, I suspect, it is a partial producer of at least some of the others. Addressing it, therefore, will most likely give us a powerful shove in the right direction. The confusion, or perhaps an even better word would be contradiction, involved has to do with our on-going efforts to improve the bottom line. Essentially, it has to do with the relationship between the cost-cutting and productivity-increasing measures used to generate more plenty. My premise is that our activities in this arena are frequently self-defeating in that they inhibit satisfaction of the most basic employee need of all, the one discussed at length in Chapter 2 and again in Chapter 7. I am, of course, talking about the need for continuity, or, more specifically, the need for physical security that is a major part of our need for continuity. By way of review, we have said that satisfaction of this need is of primary importance because physical security is essential to survival, and without survival development obviously cannot take place.

When we relate this need for physical security to our working lives, we are talking about job security. Until this is assured, the rest of our work-related needs remain secondary. Job security, in turn, generally depends on the financial health of the organization. It is at this point in our efforts to discover the best way to ensure and improve our organization's financial health that our priorities too frequently become confused, that we end up making short-sighted sacrifices that hurt us in the long run.

Let me begin this way. The things that affect a corporation's profitability can be divided roughly into two interdependent categories, one labeled "external" and the other labeled "internal." The external category includes variables in the company's environment that are largely uncontrollable. It includes such things as high interest rates, a large national deficit, union demands, changing values, workforce makeup, evolving technology, market saturation, and government regulation. The second category includes internal variables that affect a company's ability to function profitably. It includes technologies, employee attitudes, management style, communication systems, incentive systems, and work design. Most of the variables in this latter category are controllable, or at least influenceable.

The factor I am planning to address has to do with the way in which most managers manipulate internal variables in their attempt to effectively increase the amount of plenty generated. Schools of thought have been cropping up regularly in reaction to this challenge since Frederick Taylor, whom we have mentioned earlier, developed his concept of scientific management during the late 1800s. Taylor believed, for example, that the less thinking workers do, the more effective they will be at their jobs, and, therefore, the more profit they will help produce. Eventually, however, it became obvious that Taylor had left something important out of his formula. Specifically, he had overlooked the fact that employees are human beings, or "purposeful systems," as Ackoff and Emery say in their book, *On Purposeful Systems*, who are striving during working hours to achieve individual objectives as well as those defined by the company, and that they function much more effectively if treated as such. This discovery helped generate the humanist movement in the workplace.

Our next lesson was that everyone loses when our concern for the individual employee is allowed to overshadow our concern for the bottom line. As a result of this lesson, we began looking for the right degree of balance between corporate and employee control. We also began to understand that employees function better when they are told how they fit into the big picture, and when their efforts are integrated in a systemic way with appropriate technology. Finally, our most recent lesson has been that the Japanese seem to know something we don't know. They have somehow been able to satisfy employee needs and at the same time to make large industries operate in a more efficient manner, while we continue to search for the right formula.

All sorts of rationalizations have popped up in response to this latest lesson. "They don't have our problems," we say. "They're a more homogeneous population. Their culture places service to the group above self-interest. Due to a lack of natural resources, they know that they must work together in order to survive."

The appropriate reply to the above is, "Rubbish." The main reason that the Japanese are faring better than we has little to do with culture. Rather, it is, indeed, because they understand something that many of us still do not.

Our proof for this rather aggressive statement is simple. Despite our nation's "cultural handicaps," there are U.S. firms in a wide range of markets, both traditional and new, that are doing extremely well, just as well as the Japanese or anyone else on the block. The reason for their success, we can be assured, is not that they have screened employees for Japanese-like qualities. Rather, it is because they understand, logically or intuitively, a rather simple argument, one that the Japanese also understand but that many of our executives have missed.

The argument starts with our original problem: How do we improve the bottom line? The answer is that there are two ways. The *first* is by increasing income more rapidly than expenses. The most common path to increased income is through increased productivity.

We increase productivity, in turn, by improving our technology, but more important, by encouraging employees to perform at higher levels.

The *second* way to improve the bottom line is by cutting costs while keeping gross income levels steady, or at least having them drop more slowly than cost levels. We do this by weeding out duplication of effort, by defining more efficient ways to move through process steps, or by paying contractors to complete parts of the operation we are not as well-equipped to complete. What is key to my argument in terms of this second approach is that most cost-cutting efforts currently involve eliminating jobs, and when jobs are eliminated employees are usually released.

Which one of these approaches to improving the bottom line do most U.S. managers take? Which do they generally find most applicable to their situation? The answer to this question is "both." Both are going on at the same time. On the one hand, managers are starting up employee councils, quality circles, safety committees, semiautonomous work groups, and other participative management vehicles. On the other hand, they are hiring efficiency experts to explore ways to cut jobs and salaries out of various departments, decrease hierarchical levels, and replace employees with machines.

This dual approach, I believe, is at least one of the keys to Management U.S.A.'s dilemma. It is a major source of our confusion, our inability to continually improve the bottom line, and to ensure our access to the developmental input of plenty as well as to that of good. It is, in many respects, *the* problem, the one we must deal with first. It is also a key producer of those things we had previously considered *the* problem. They, it turns out, were for the most part merely symptoms.

"But why?" we hear. "Why can't we do both at once? The two approaches are complementary, aren't they? The objective of both is to improve the bottom line, isn't it?"

Yes. On the most obvious level they complement one another. The objective of both is, indeed, to improve the bottom line, one by increasing productivity, the other by cutting costs. But when we delve a little deeper, it rapidly becomes obvious that the two approaches are, in fact, anything but complementary.

The logic for this argument proceeds as follows. First, in order to improve the bottom line by increasing productivity, we have to improve the performance level of employees. Upgrading technology is also important, but if one has to choose, the employee effort should take precedence. As we all know, wonders are accomplished daily by dedicated workers when the technology at their disposal is minimal or even primitive. On the other hand, the most sophisticated technology in the world cannot compensate for a sloppy, disenchanted, or absent operator.

How do we improve the performance of employees? We accomplish this by offering them rewards they value in return for their greater efforts. One major reward besides salary is our much discussed respect. "I want respect for the fact that I know my job and can help improve things. Ask my opinion. No one knows better than I what goes on in my own area of expertise." By far the most important such reward, however, when we get down to basics is, of course, the reward of continuity in terms of our physical security, in terms of our paycheck. It is the reward that we seek before all else. "Let *me* decide when I'm leaving. Don't disrupt my life. Job security is the thing I value most. When it is assured, I can begin looking for ways to improve the quality of both my work and my working environment. Without it, however, I'm not going to do as well."

"Okay," you say, "that makes sense. I agree."

"But wait a minute," I say. "Haven't we forgotten something? What about the second prong of our strategy to improve earnings? What about the efficiency experts? What have they been up to?"

"The efficiency experts?" you frown. "What have they been up to? It's obvious what they've been up to, isn't it? They've been getting rid of the dead wood. Now see here, this job security thing's fine, and we'll get to it. But first we have to make sure that the operation is efficient. Anyway, every job that we eliminate automatically improves the bottom line and makes things better for those who are left. That's our main objective, isn't it? The efficiency experts are producing immediate savings. Look at those figures. You can't argue with them."

No, we can't. Not in the short term, at least. So both approaches do seem to have merit. Both, at one point or another, have led to improvement in the bottom line. The problem is, however, that they cannot exist successfully together. In order for either one to succeed, the other, almost by definition, cannot be a serious consideration.

This statement is critical to our argument and needs elaboration. Conflict, we believe, between the job security/participation approach and the current efficiency expert approach is unavoidable. The first succeeds by relating to employees as reasoning beings who will react positively to the right stimulation and improve their performance, while the second succeeds by viewing employees as our previously-discussed numbers on a tally sheet to be manipulated and crossed out at will based on financial considerations. The first encourages a new world mentality, while the second reinforces all the aforementioned impediments to progress. It takes control away from people. It views technology as a replacement for rather than a means of freeing workers for higher levels of effort and achievement. It reinforces conflict as well as the need for political machinations by forcing us to focus once again on the issue of individual survival. Finally, due to its short-term perspective with dollars and cents as the only accepted measure of success, it discourages the exploration and generation of other types of rewards.

The point I am trying to make is that it is impossible to get employees to take seriously promises of increased access to good, of job security, of increased participation and training opportunities, and to have them focus on improving productivity when they see efficiency experts prowling about in the shadows. They balk. Their attention is riveted. They know that, deep down, management is still out to get them. All the rest is just a ruse to distract them. They feel helpless. They feel angry. They do not feel like putting out the extra effort necessary to increase productivity. They have been suckered too many times already. They are definitely not about to get a fair deal.

As an obvious result of such frequently well-founded suspicions, the productivity-increasing part of this dual approach doesn't work. Because the productivity-increasing part doesn't work or stimulates only marginal improvement, more cost-cutting studies and measures are necessary. But as more efficiency-related heads roll, employee morale, commitment, and productivity continue to drop, so that savings from cost-cutting measures are offset by further productivity decreases. At this point more cost cutting becomes necessary in order for the company to survive. And so on as the progression degenerates into a vicious cycle.

My conclusion, then, is that while the current efficiency expert approach usually leads to short-term improvement in the bottom line, in the long run, due to its lack of regard for basic developmental needs of the most important and volatile asset any corporation has—the employee as a human being—it inevitably will produce a no-win situation. What the Japanese and a growing number of progressive

U.S. corporations understand is that any serious effort to improve the bottom line must begin by encouraging a sense of commitment and trust in the people who create that line, and that the first step toward this end must be the assurance of job security, of continuity, and, ultimately, of good in their working lives.

On a societal level, the pursuit of good historically has been a major, if not *the* major, issue in our nation's evolution. Many of our early settlers left Europe to escape intolerance. The framers of our Constitution, greatly influenced by Enlightenment period thinking, declared that men are created equal and that, as the Greeks had said, those who settled here should enjoy the right to life, liberty, and the pursuit of happiness. Our nation's focus was to be on facilitating human and societal development and on providing those inputs necessary to the realization of individual and societal potential. One of the vehicles reinforcing this mentality was the free enterprise system. Success in the free enterprise system, by definition, depends on the realization of potential. But the free enterprise system also has a darker side. This, of course, is its tendency to encourage conflict, to encourage beating and taking advantage of the other guy or gal. Many of the men who actually helped write our Constitution were, curiously enough, slaveholders and, as such, allowed their actions to contradict their declarations. The problem was that while most of them believed at least theoretically in the universal provision of good, they also espoused and believed strongly in free enterprise as the most efficient mechanism for developing the nation's resources and for making plenty available.

They were right. Free enterprise is, indeed, the most effective mechanism that we know. At the same time, however, it has led to the loss of life, liberty, the pursuit of happiness, and a fair deal for many. This, however, has occurred, in my opinion, not because ours is a seriously flawed system, but because our definitional emphasis has been in the wrong place. Once again we find ourselves doing a balancing act. In order to succeed we must discover an appropriate answer to the critical question, "How do we produce the good promised all our citizens by the Constitution, while, at the same time, keep free enterprise and its incentives alive?"

Traditionally, the legal profession has been saddled with this responsibility. Sometimes it has been effective, sometimes it has not. Lawyers have proven themselves just as vulnerable to the lure of financial gain as anyone else, which is regrettable but certainly understandable. All too often they have been willing to compromise their professional values in its pursuit. The need for lawyers in our society is actually a created need rather than a natural one. The natural need that we are talking about is for an accepted code of behavior that facilitates societal development, and for a viable means of settling disputes.

In other countries, based on such a code, agreements are made vocally, sealed with a handshake, and honored, largely because to not honor them would lead to a loss of societal and self-respect. In our culture, all too frequently, respect plays no role. Agreements are written in extremely detailed legalese to prevent the other guy or gal from finding a loophole. They are then carefully monitored, the thought being that the opposition will begin looking for ways to break or misinterpret them almost as soon as the ink is dry. In other countries arbitrators handle disputes, most being settled out of court. In ours, we need a battery of lawyers and years of litigation to dig through the morass of arguments and counter-arguments that rage among various corporations, between the business and consumer worlds, and between the business world and regulatory agencies.

The resources and energy allocated to such "defensive" activities, the money and man-hours invested in preparing accusations and denials are the negative expenditures since their contribution to development is minimal at best. At the same time, they burden us with a cost that many of our competitors in the world marketplace avoid, thus putting us at a disadvantage. When we adopt the development ethic, however, such waste will become more obvious and less necessary. When our perspective expands in terms of what we want from life, when it moves away from plenty, which is generally what lawyers bicker over, we will assume a more positive focus concerning the value and expenditure of both societal and personal resources. As a result, the legal profession will shrink in both size and importance. Good will supercede winning as our objective, and we will move more rapidly toward the kind of institutional and individual relationships that our forefathers and their tutors, the Enlightenment period thinkers, had in mind when they sat down to create a nation.

The development ethic will also bring about changes in our criminal justice system. There are two approaches to the prevention of crime. The first I call the "after-the-fact-stop-it-from-happening-again" approach. Advocates of this school try to identify, apprehend, and arrest criminals, then to either change their behavior or to isolate them from society. Ways of doing the above include improving communication among law enforcement agencies, doing studies that identify the characteristics of chronic repeaters so that they are not endlessly flushed back onto the streets, rehabilitating, building new jails, and voting for capital punishment.

The second approach I call the "before-the-fact-eliminate-the-producers" approach. Advocates of this school try to identify and rectify, or at least counteract, the societal forces that help shape criminals. The Police Athletic League is a familiar example of such an effort, as are the numerous social agencies focusing on reaching, redirecting, and training the underprivileged for more productive careers.

According to reports, neither of these approaches seems to be succeeding. The weakness of the first is that it obviously does little about the producers of crime. It is generally agreed that crime is more a result of nurture than of nature. Genetics, or physical imperfections, obviously play a role in some cases, but the percentage of such instances is relatively small. Most criminals become what they are because at some point, usually early in life, they are misguided or are left to survive as best they can with no guidance at all. With the above in mind, therefore, even if we were able to jail 100 percent of today's criminals, our relief would probably be short-lived. The forces responsible for their conditioning would still be lurking in the shadows out there.

The second, "before-the-fact-eliminate-the-producers" approach, in turn, is hamstrung by a lack of necessary resources. The question yet to be answered satisfactorily is, "How can concerned parties possibly counteract the effects of an almost totally negative environment?" For example, how do we negate the joint impact of poor housing; of role models that exude failure and defeat; of a lousy diet since infancy; of little or no education; of extremely limited employment opportunity; and, finally, of a subculture where the physically strong continue to prey on everyone else? Several hours a day in a gym or a weekly visit by the neighborhood social worker, no matter how sincere he or she might be, is not usually going to make that much of a difference.

It is obviously necessary, therefore, to look for another alternative in our efforts to eradicate crime, one built on a different and broader perspective. The alternative I have in mind I would call the "make-crime-meaningless" approach.

In order to understand this third approach, we will first have to talk about the nature of crime itself. One way of making my desired point is by saying that there are three types of nonviolent crime. The first I would call "experimental." The experimental criminal is frequently young and is testing the system, seeing if it really is wrong to "take something that doesn't belong to me," seeing if "I really will be punished if they catch me." Experimental criminals usually outgrow their penchant to break the law. Most such offenses are petty in nature and have little impact on our economy. The shoplifting of candy, toys, and so forth by minors is a common example of experimental crime.

The second type I would call "subsistence-level" nonviolent crime. It is committed by people who cannot satisfy their survival needs through normal channels. This class of criminal includes those who earn only minimum wage when they have three children to support. It includes those who have tried but cannot find work and are on welfare. If salary or benefits are insufficient or are mismanaged so that the recipient runs out of funds before the next check arrives, or if the income is stolen either directly or indirectly by landlords, merchants, or friends, such people might view crime as the only remaining way to obtain the inputs necessary to life.

In this vein, I read a story a while ago about an old woman caught hiding two cans of dog food beneath her coat while trying to pass through a checkout point in a grocery store. During her interrogation it came out that she had been existing on dog food for quite some time. "It doesn't really taste that bad," she said smiling, and besides, it was all she could afford. That month, however, a foul-up had occurred at the agency and her check hadn't arrived on time, so she had been forced to either steal or go hungry. This woman's crime obviously fits into our subsistence-level category.

Another group we should place in this category is the growing number of addicts driven by their habit to steal in order to afford the necessary cocaine, heroin, crack, or alcohol. While the need involved is not natural, it is by all means just as critical as any other, according to the addict's perception of survival.

The third type of nonviolent crime in my classification I would label "situation-improvement" crime. One group of people who commit such offenses are kids and adults who have been taught that crime is an acceptable occupation. Entire families are frequently involved in such operations. Parents teach children the tools of their trade. Fathers and sons, mothers and daughters work as teams. Organized crime, of course, is a well-known example of this type.

This category also includes the growing number of nonaddicted drug dealers in our nation and world.

Finally, it includes white-collar criminals, employees who find ways to steal from employers, frequently with the aid of computers, because they are not satisfied with their salaries and benefits, or because they are deeply in debt and see this as the only way of getting out of it.

In sum, then, the situation-improvement category includes all those not worried about survival but, at the same time, who aren't happy with their current portion of the existing wealth and break the law in order to add to it. This category is by far the largest. Its origin is our struggle over plenty as the most important input to the good life. Emphasis is on fourth-level achievement, the other three types not being a serious consideration. Emphasis is also entirely on image as opposed to content. The criminal certainly can't expect to be respected for his or her deeds except, perhaps, by fellow criminals, so ill-gotten gains are spent largely on impression pieces. Situation-improving criminals, in fact, are frequently caught this way because they are spending more than they can possibly afford to on their legitimate income.

Most nonviolent crimes and a good percentage of the violent crimes committed are, in fact, a result of the reality that we have kept in place by depending on outdated definitions. Once those definitions have been reworked, crime, as we know it, should subside.

I imagine that for many readers the above statement is going to be rather hard to accept, especially when one remembers that thousands and thousands of police, criminologists, judges, social workers, and parole officers have thus far made very little difference. To announce that a few definitional changes should eventually do the trick might seem an extremely naive gesture. But think about it. There are very few developmental crimes. One does not generally steal physical fitness, wisdom, or emotional stability. One might have to steal the money required to gain admittance to a fitness center, to a college, or to a psychiatrist's office, but not so much and not so frequently as when the coveted items are expensive impression pieces. At the same time, if things work as they are supposed to in our society, appropriate amounts of justice, beauty, and control over one's destiny should be available free of charge. Once we shift our emphasis away from the acquisition of plenty and what it affords us, therefore, and onto other development-related accomplishments and inputs, once we have defined these other accomplishments and inputs as being just as critical to the achievement of self- and societal respect as wealth, there should not be as much situation-improving crime. The things it makes available will no longer suffice. Such crime will no longer provide a shortcut to the desired ultimate reward.

Our move into the new world should also have a marked effect on subsistence-level crime. For one thing, as we have said in Chapter 10, our approach to the eradication of poverty, from which such crime springs, will become more comprehensive and effective. We will be less tolerant of poverty's existence and will take the measures necessary to eradicate it. Concerning the addicts we have included in this category, due to our more balanced perspective many of the work-related forces driving these people to alcohol and drugs will disappear, or at least diminish. At the same time, the image value of, say, snorting cocaine will not be as great because such activity will be anathematic to the concept of development. Finally, with our greater emphasis on good and our decreased emphasis on plenty, we will deal more severely with dealers. They will have less opportunity to buy their way out of trouble.

In summary, then, we see that when the acquisition and provision of good become equal in importance to the acquisition and provision of plenty, both in the workplace and on the street, life will become more secure and safe, as well as better balanced and richer.

13

BEAUTY BREAKS LOOSE

The pursuit of beauty, according to the ancient Greek philosophers, as we have said in Chapter 7, concerns our quest for contentment and excitement in life, contentment resulting from a pleasing, non-threatening work and leisure environment that soothes the senses, and excitement resulting from the availability of challenge, newness, and adventure to stimulate the senses. It's obvious that the ideal, as defined, relates to our initial needs framework introduced in Chapter 2. There we outlined our existence in terms of the need for continuity and the balancing need for change. What we were talking about, it seems, could be considered the aesthetics of life, those ingredients that make our days enjoyable.

If we are to achieve aesthetic satisfaction in life, however, it is necessary for us to understand that the concept of *environment*, in this instance at least, includes our *activities* as well as our *surroundings*. It is necessary for us to seek beauty in both. For example, we can occupy the most spacious, nicely furnished office in the city, but if our job is to stare at a word processing or computer screen all day long, something is lacking. In our leisure life, we can live in a grand house in a fine neighborhood, but if we don't have anything in common with our neighbors, something is missing.

The objective in terms of our pursuit of beauty, then, is for us to find in both our working and leisure lives contentment and stimulation, and to find them in terms of our activities as well as our surroundings.

Let's begin with our workplace setting. We will talk first about our external surroundings, then our internal ones. In terms of our external workplace surroundings, a growing number of corporate headquarters seem to be moving out of city skyscrapers and to more rural locations. The reasons for such moves include aesthetic considerations as well as steadily increasing taxes and high rents. While one finds plenty of stimulation in the city setting, it is not always of a beneficial nature. For example, the streets of Manhattan are so stimulating that one learns quickly to avoid speaking to or responding to strangers. At the same time, it is usually difficult to find contentment in an urban setting, to be soothed, due to the constant wash of noise, people, pollution, and changing visual impressions. Because of such imbalance, our aesthetic gratification is, at best, lopsided and, as a result, does not meet our developmental requirements.

When we move to a more rural setting, external shortcomings are usually countered. The amount of negative sensual stimulation obviously diminishes, while chances for a soothing environment increase greatly. The problem is that we usually do not take advantage of these chances, or are not allowed to. I have been in a number of corporate headquarters buildings with windows that look out over acres and acres of well-maintained, unused grounds. Employees walk or jog on them before work and during lunch hour, but that's about it. I once stood in the first floor corner office of a vice president of human resources that had two glass walls looking out onto an upward sloping embankment. When I mentioned the view, the vice president said, "Yes, it was very peaceful, wasn't it?" He wished there was a door so he could sneak out occasionally. In terms of getting out, however, he couldn't even open the windows. They were hermetically sealed. The building had a self-contained and totally self-controlled environment. He smiled, "No one escapes."

Another time I visited a headquarters building that had terraces on all floors. Every door that I tried, however, except the one leading to the terrace off the cafeteria, was locked. I was told that they had to be locked for security reasons. A shallow lake had been dug into the front lawn of this building and a fountain installed. Again, acres of grass stretched out in all directions. Very scenic and well tended, except that there was a problem. The problem was Canadian geese.

A large number of them had apparently taken up residence on and around the lake, befouling its waters and clogging the fountain's filter system.

Just about everyone I talked with eventually mentioned this problem, although I never saw any of the villains myself. The lawns stayed empty, except for the maintenance crew. Then, one spring evening a session ran well past quitting time. The sun was setting when I left the building. The sky was deep, tarnished gold and pink and a rich blue fading slowly. The air was cool and crisp, but with a lingering warmth and tinge of dampness to it. As I drove out of the parking lot, I heard honking. I pulled to the side of the road and got out of my car. When I looked up, I saw them coming in, long graceful Vs of geese silhouetted against the dying fire of the sky. There must have been 50 such flights, rippling and shifting, forging one after another through the shadows from different directions with a rhythmic flow of wings. As they drew closer, they began calling and circling, then wound their way slowly in to loudly claim a spot on the lake or on the nearby lawn.

It was a very pleasant sight. I stood there in the growing chill for at least a half hour, watching, feeling the peacefulness and the foreverness of the event, thinking that perhaps I had not seen the geese at their worst, but I had now most certainly seen them at their best. At the same time, I wondered how many of the people who worked here had witnessed this spectacle, or, perhaps, were even capable of noticing that something unusual might be happening, for, while I lingered, a number of cars hurried by, headed for the exit, not even slowing except for the drivers to glance curiously at me.

Based on these two experiences and more like them, my impression is that, in terms of the aesthetic pleasures offered by our external work surroundings, no matter how plentiful they might be, too many of us are "driving by too quickly" to take advantage of or perhaps even to notice them. We are hermetically sealed into our work lives, unable to get outside. Sometimes, in fact, due to our lack of a balanced perspective, as we have said earlier, we actually draw the blinds, afraid that the view might prove too appealing, might be too distracting. For reasons discussed, it appears that we too often consider our external surroundings, when they are pleasing, more of a corporate impression piece than a potential source of nourishment.

The same problem, basically, crops up when we talk about the aesthetics of our internal work surroundings. Barren and sterile are two adjectives frequently used. Yet, despite regulations, despite tattle tales and reprimands, people are constantly trying to sneak in personal touches, to add a little color and warmth to their offices or space with family pictures, cartoons scotch-taped onto the walls, an unauthorized plant on the window sill, an unusual trashcan, a miniature basketball hoop to throw wadded-up paper balls through.

Usually, however, employees at every level below that of the presidency are very careful about how far they go. I have been in presidents' offices that showed a lot about the character and taste of the man or woman. Exercise equipment, pieces from private art collections, antique furnishings brought from home, golf clubs, foreign language newspapers and magazines on the desk, classic fiction on the bookshelves along with technical materials—these are examples of what I have found.

With vice presidents, however, and everyone else, emphasis remains on maintaining the right image, on not taking any chances, on not giving in-house competition anything that can be cast in a negative light. The mind-set is that we have been given the tools necessary for our efforts. Anything else we introduce into our environment is superfluous and a potential threat to efficiency, leaving us open to question.

The best alternative in this situation is to be as much like everyone else as possible. Sameness, it seems, is one of the keys to job security. In our defensiveness, we frequently even dress the same way. In *Problem Solving for Managers* I mentioned what I call the "grey pinstripe syndrome," the propensity of our executives to wear grey suits. I heartily dislike the color grey for that reason. It is the color of metal, of machine parts, and machine parts are inanimate, insensitive, uncreative objects. A fellow consultant, a friend of mine, once sat in a board room at the conclusion of a successful design project. During the conversation following his presentation he told me that someone had asked casually how he would redesign the board function, if asked to. My friend had replied, half in jest, that the first thing he would do would be to suggest that everyone show up for work tomorrow wearing different colored suits. No one had laughed. No one had even smiled. It had obviously been the wrong thing to say. My friend believed that some of those present had actually felt offended by his suggestion. He had later been told that several of the board members had found his directness at least indiscrete.

The symbolic implications of our grey pinstriped corporate world, however, are too obvious for anyone concerned with aesthetics and the pursuit of beauty to ignore. They take us back to our previous discussion of the image-content continuum. The image end of this continuum, as we have said, is not all bad. It is bad only when we focus exclusively, or in too unbalanced a manner on it and pay inadequate attention to content. When kept in perspective, however, it does serve a valuable function. This function is to help give us an identity both as an individual and as a group member. The way we dress, speak, and carry ourselves can tell people what our talents are. If we are good athletes, for example, and have well-developed bodies, we wear shorts and T-shirts to advertise this fact. If we are artists, we decorate ourselves with make-up and jewelry, showing our ability to combine color and fabric in unusual ways, and frequently perform instead of just carrying on conversations.

What is the message of the grey flannel suit group? To me, it begins with, "Hey, look at us. We are extensions of technology. We are proud of what technology has accomplished, so we dress to show our kinship to it." At the same time, however, it includes, "Hey, look at us. See how dull we are. Because we dress and function like machine parts, we don't need to think creatively, to be excited by the unusual or the unknown. We just have to keep grinding it out in the same, steady, old way, and everything will be fine."

The key word in the above, of course, is "creatively." This is a theme of growing importance to our corporations. Technology is the historic result of our desire to increase the efficiency of production, to manufacture more parts, and to provide more services for less cost to both the producer and the customer. The essence of efficiency, once the best process has been defined, is repetition. Companies, in their attempts to succeed, have traditionally stressed this repetition, or again, sameness in employee as well as technical systems.

In terms of efficiency, however, the problem we must currently address is that serious changes have occurred in the world of business since our search for it first began. For one thing, the variables that maintain and increase efficiency are much more a given than they used to be. Corporations, for example, have a harder time keeping their technological improvements secret. When someone comes up with something new, everyone else has figured it out or borrowed it and is also reaping the benefits within a year or so.

As a result of this change and others, we have begun looking for another edge, another way to make ourselves more attractive, and this new edge or way of enhancing our appeal has been identified as creativity. Rather than continually refining the current process or product, rather than continually seeking ways to cut costs, we are beginning to look for novel ways of putting the pieces together. As a result of this shift, the questions we are starting to pay the most attention to in the workplace are, "How do we come up with something original? How do we generate creativity? How do we stimulate our employees to think in a creative manner?" rather than, "How can we continue to get more for less? How do we cut out another step?"

My answer to these new, critical questions is, again, that many of the necessary changes will occur when we adopt the development ethic. The development ethic encourages the exploration of individual potential and, therefore, uniqueness, rather than the similarity we have traditionally striven for. Being unique and thinking uniquely can result in creativity. The professional group in our society that goes to the greatest lengths to express its uniqueness is also, by no accident, that group considered the most creative. I am, of course, talking about our artists, actors, film makers, and so on. These people show their uniqueness in many ways, but one of the most obvious, as we have said, is through dress. They are usually the most distinctive and flamboyant dressers around.

If the business sector truly wants to inspire creativity within its ranks, therefore, it should perhaps take a hint. It should allow another bad habit to bite the dust and give employees more control over what they wear. It should begin encouraging employees to express their individuality, their uniqueness through dress, and eventually also through how they decorate and organize their work space.

The above changes would obviously not have much of an effect on the business culture as a whole. They are in no way the answer to the problem we are trying to address. What they would provide, however, is a starting point, a small but positive step in the right direction. They would not only make the workforce more comfortable and improve office or shop aesthetics, but they would also help define a new, more individualistic and creative mood in terms of the overall operation, one that, hopefully, would take root and produce new shoots.

A second way that I can think of to stimulate creativity in the workplace has to do chiefly with the aesthetics of our activities. Our current responsibilities usually reflect the same disregard for individual developmental needs that our dress and decorating codes do. A great difference, we have seen, exists between contentment and boredom, between peacefulness and repetition. Contentment does not come from an absence of challenge. Rather, it comes from enjoying our work, from doing it well, from learning continuously from it, and finally, from being stimulated by it.

By way of elaboration, we are all involved in two types of workplace activities. The first includes our individual tasks. Do we formulate reference projections and scenarios? Do we take notes at meetings? Do we contribute to problem-solving efforts? Do we write or give reports, analyze material, push buttons, and watch dials? We have already, in Chapter 3, discussed a way in which these tasks can be categorized and compared, and where emphasis should lie once we have adopted the development ethic and begun to use technology the way it should be used. For one thing, in terms of the individual, as we have indicated earlier, when machines take over increasing numbers of the repetitive functions in primary production and service industries, more people will become involved in R&D efforts, a type of developmental work that will benefit the bottom line while, at the same time, unleashing individual creativity and improving the aesthetics of employee efforts by providing stimulation and challenge.

The second type of activity includes those tasks that necessitate interaction with others. The makeup of the groups we join and participate in on a daily or periodic basis greatly affects the aesthetics of our working life. Traditionally, of course, here also we adhere to the clone principle. We frequently try to stack teams with members who think like us, who look like us, who understand us and don't make too many waves. Sameness, again, is the safest and most efficient route.

I was once involved in a research project at a large telecommunications firm. We studied the personality characteristics of a class of rising stars—a class of young managers picked by superiors because of their potential for further grooming. The personality typology we based our work on had four categories. The results of our study showed that 72 percent of our subjects fell into the same category, and it was not one that stressed creativity.

Later, I was involved in a second research project. Our purpose here was to discover which of these four personality categories or which personality type combination was the most creative. The important results of this second project, however, were not what we had expected. Our most relevant finding, it turned out, was not that one type or pair of types proved more creative than the others. Rather, as we have indicated earlier in this chapter and in others, it was that the greater the variety of personality types you have on a team, the more creative your results are going to be.

The above discovery, of course, is not surprising. It is, in fact, quite obvious and quite common-sensical. If members of a group all bring the same thing to a project, the results are not going to be as rich as they will if everyone brings something different. An acceptable answer to the problem addressed, an acceptable compromise or synthesis, of course, will take longer to achieve in the latter situation. There will be more disagreements to work through, more argument, more ideas to consider. One negative consequence of this quest for more varied input obviously will be that a degree of efficiency, a greater amount of time will be sacrificed during the process. But what we get in exchange for this loss is also obvious. It will be a more comprehensive and probably more creative solution at a time when creativity is replacing efficiency as our primary corporate consideration.

In summary, then, adoption of the development ethic in the workplace will help improve the aesthetics of both our surroundings and our activities. It will add more variety and more stimulation in terms of what we see, hear, and think about. It will provide more contentment as well, by contributing to the developmental needs of employees. Finally, and perhaps most important in the short run, it will help encourage the generation of creative responses to both corporate and noncorporate challenges.

The quest for beauty in our leisure lives, the second major focus of this chapter, is certainly not new. Every normal person wants access to surroundings and activities that can provide a feeling of peacefulness and harmony as well as stimulation when desired. We obviously have more control over our activities during leisure hours. The trade-offs we make here are based largely on our own decisions. Let us talk mainly, then, about our surroundings. We all like a home that expresses our individuality. We all like tree-lined streets; neat, lush lawns to walk past, if not to maintain; we all like the sight of a well-tended garden; of wooded areas with a babbling stream running through; of open fields covered with tall, golden grasses and wildflowers. No one that I know of likes the constant roar and blare of traffic. No one likes sunsets blurred by smog. No one likes a disfigured, barren landscape littered with trash.

But if we all feel pretty much the same way, why do we continue to do things that disrupt the aesthetics of our leisure environment? What is the problem? There are, of course, magnificent monuments to man's love of beauty. Whole cities and towns like Venice; Zermott; Charleston, South Carolina; and Carmel, California are examples. Buildings like Notre Dame, St. Peter's Cathedral, and Frank Lloyd Wright's Falling Water are also examples of this love, as are parks like Yellowstone and the Everglades and privately owned lands like the farm country of the Shenandoah Valley. At the same time, however, efforts must continually be made to guard these well-loved national treasures against encroachment. Industries are spewing forth pollution that threatens literally to dissolve the beauty of entire cities. Acid rain is quite possibly decimating our forests. Our society is full of developers who would not hesitate one minute to chop into the Yellowstone, or to dynamite the cliffs along the California coast, or to drain the Everglades completely if they thought that a profit could be made.

Many of these happenings can be attributed to a deep-rooted, bad habit. This habit, another leftover from earlier days, is our continuing tendency to think of nature as something to be conquered, as a slave of man to be drained of its energy, stripped and milked of its resources, then discarded. Some people blame this attitude on our religious heritage. For example, there are some verses in the Bible that can be interpreted as justifying, if not encouraging, man's frequent disrespect for his natural surroundings. These can be and have been used as excuses for our short-sightedness. The main culprit, however, in my mind, is again probably history.

The reasoning behind my suspicion goes like this. During earlier periods of man's and society's evolutions, nature was very much an enemy that had to be conquered if we were to wrest from it those things necessary to physical survival and safety. Dangerous animals had to be hunted and tamed. Differentiation had to be made between edible and poisonous plants. Natural diseases capable of wiping out entire populations had to be confronted. Weather was one of the biggest challenges. Drought, for example, historically has caused a great amount of suffering and death and still obviously remains to be conquered, as we see from what is happening in North Africa. Other natural forces that continue to wreak havoc on man's developmental efforts are hurricanes, earthquakes, and tidal waves. I doubt that there are very many people, conservation-minded or not, who wouldn't applaud the conquest of these continuing reminders of nature's awesome power and disrespect.

Even when nature behaves, however, wrestling from it what is necessary for survival can be difficult. As we see from such films as Bergman's "The Immigrants" and the more recent "Places In The Heart," from such books as Pearl Buck's *The Good Earth* and Steinbeck's *The Grapes of Wrath*, simply gaining enough to eat has probably been history's greatest challenge.

When we add our own mistakes and misunderstandings to nature's frequent reticence to cooperate, the situation becomes even more critical. In the United States examples of how this combined misunderstanding and reticence can threaten our survival are being explained to us with increasing frequency by scientists, environmentalists, and other concerned groups. Barry Commoner's account in *The Closing Circle* of nature's inability to absorb and break down all the waste that we are generating, especially waste containing new molecular compounds created in our laboratories, is a classic. The pollution of ground water and our on-going tendency to pave over and build on some of the world's most productive farm land are other examples.

The point is that while our relationship with nature has improved, while much of her threat has been eliminated and many of the problems limiting our ability to tap into her wealth have been overcome, we still, in many instances, continue to treat her as the enemy. No injury done her is too grievous, no insult too great. She is out to get us, so we should take her for everything we can, then clear out and not worry about the long-term consequences. As we see, in terms of this perhaps most critical relationship, our previously discussed, outdated conflict mentality continues to dominate and to shape our perspective, even though the negative implications of our stubbornness are becoming increasingly obvious and increasingly frightening.

What we need again, then, to bring about the necessary change in attitude on the necessary scale is a new frame of reference. This new frame, according to my perspective, of course, is the development ethic. Once our conversion to the development ethic has helped us achieve a better balance in terms of our values, I believe that we will be less likely to continue viewing nature as something to be conquered, and more likely to view her as a valuable partner, one never to be trusted completely, but one that is both essential and an unmatched and irreplaceable resource in our efforts to meet the full range of our developmental needs.

The above argument concerns the extreme in terms of our disrespect for our environment. In most cases, indeed, we understand the interdependence that we share with nature, the fact that we must take care of her and literally cannot survive without her. Yet, even here, a strange and somewhat irrational double standard frequently seems to exist. In terms of industry, for example, the same corporate board members, presidents, vice presidents, directors, foremen, and hourly workers who have lovely gardens and yards that they take great pride in maintaining during off hours feed the smokestacks and drainage ditches that spew forth pollutants. It's as though their private lives are totally divorced from their work lives. While in the former they seek tranquility and beauty, in the latter their values shift radically. At work sacrifices have to be made, and the environment is an unavoidable victim. "We don't *want* to dump this stuff out there, but we *have* to in order to stay competitive. People worried about the survival of the environment just don't *understand* the pressures to which corporate decision makers are subject." The major concern in the mind of the employee, as opposed to gardener, is, as we have said, to make as much money as possible in return for all those hours, days, months, and years spent at situation-improving work because few other rewards are available. If the environment gets bruised in the process, it's regrettable but unavoidable.

Once we switch to the development ethic we should be better able to temper this reality. Once our quest for beauty in life becomes more equally balanced with that for plenty and once a majority of the available jobs become developmental rather than situation-improving in nature, we will question more seriously our willingness to trade long-term aesthetic satisfaction for a short-term or even monetary "win." When profits and the bottom line are no longer our sole motivators, corporations and stockholders will be more willing to spend or do what is necessary to protect the beauty created by both man and nature, the beauty off of which we feed.

This change of attitude will be further encouraged by our realization that a growing number of jobs can be done just as effectively or even more effectively in the home or at sites other than the office. As a result of this shift away from the corporate headquarters building, central office, or the factory, three things should happen. First, we will become more attuned to our external environment and, therefore, will be less likely to shrug off the poor pollution control practices of both public and private sector organizations as unavoidable. In essence, the connection between our highly prized gardens and lawns and the rest of the environment will become increasingly obvious. Second, we will see the positive effects relatively simple changes in our work routine that are nonharmful to overall corporate objectives can produce on the aesthetic quality of our lives and will be more likely to begin seeking ways to make further improvements. An obvious example of such a change will be the decrease in commuting time. As a result of this decrease we will gain control over additional hours, those previously spent on trains or in the car. Simultaneously, the levels of pollution, noise, frustration, and highway construction we encounter daily will most likely drop due to the decrease in rush hour congestion. Finally, in many instances we will save money that can eventually be used in a more satisfying manner. Brian, our friend from Chapter 1, for example, rather than spending $145 each month for his commuter pass, will be able to bank at least part of that sum and perhaps spend it at the end of the year on a family trip to Disneyworld.

Such a trip, in most cases, would not be the only improvement in the aesthetic quality of son Eddy's and wife Cathy's lives produced by Brian's increased presence in the home during working hours. If more people telecommuted, dad and husband or mom and wife would be around to share meals, to talk with and play with during breaks, to call on during emergencies. The aesthetics of family life as a whole would improve and, hopefully, many of the previously discussed problems linked to the demise of this institution would diminish. We are now, obviously, talking about the aesthetics of activities as well as those of environment. People telecommuting would be able to improve the aesthetics of their individual, work-related activities, as well as those of their surroundings. For one thing, they would become increasingly task as opposed to time oriented. That is, their emphasis would be more on completing the assignment than on filling a certain number of hours with motion, with busy work. Also, instead of grinding straight through an eight-hour day without pause, work time could be apportioned more wisely. If dad or mom, for example, felt tired at two in the afternoon, he or she could take a nap or go for a walk and pick the project up again after dinner when fresh. Another benefit would be that regular exercise breaks could become a fact of life rather than fantasy as they are with most office-bound employees.

Finally, in response to the observation that people in such situations would or do miss the social interaction found at the office, as more neighbors began telecommuting neighborhood activities would probably become an increasingly vital part of the daily routine. I have lived in commuter communities, those in which one sees acquaintances on the block mainly while cutting the grass Saturday morning or at cocktail parties. These communities lack the flavor, the richness, and the degree of give and take found elsewhere, the interaction which is so vividly portrayed for me by the Dagwood comic strip that I read every Sunday. Perhaps our own Blondies and Herbs and Tootsies would come to life if more of us began telecommuting and would help fill the supposed void left by our decreased office interaction.

There is one more area of interest that I want to cover in this section. That is the area of the fine arts. I believe that our adoption of the development ethic will make a positive difference in our culture's attitude here as well. Because people will seek and gain increased control over their time in the new world, and because, in the same instance, they will begin to desire a more balanced realization of their potential, a portion of this additional time will be dedicated to artistic pursuits. We as individuals will begin to produce more of our own art. We will become Renaissance men and women. We will paint more of our own pictures, play more of our own music, dance more of our own dances. Perhaps we will not do these things with great skill and grace, but we will do them with enough to cultivate a richer appreciation of the nature of beauty. One of the results of this richer appreciation and increased awareness, in turn, will be that we as a population will become less susceptible to "gimmick art," fads, and hard sells. In order to raise our level of satisfaction we will become more critical in terms of what pleases us, more focused on content. As a result of this evolution, full-fledged artists will find their audiences much more knowledgeable and demanding, but, at the same time, much more appreciative when something of true value is produced.

In summary, then, adoption of the development ethic will open ways to improve the aesthetic quality of both our surroundings and activities in our leisure as well as our working lives, and will help bring these two worlds closer together by broadening our perspective and encouraging us to update our values. In other words, it will help to make our existence more enjoyable as well as more productive. When we strike a better balance between our quest for plenty and our quest for beauty, the latter will truly break loose and become an integral part of our day-to-day existence rather than an endangered treat—one we must frequently fight to protect, one we must too often watch being destroyed by those lacking the proper vision and sensitivity.

14

POWER: CORNERSTONE
OF THE NEW WORLD

It has been growing increasingly obvious as we have moved through the last four chapters that adoption of the development ethic will enhance the degree of control, or power, we all enjoy. This power, as we have said earlier, is perhaps the most critical input of all to the realization of individual and societal potential, the one without which the required and desired amounts of plenty, truth, good, and beauty frequently cannot be gained. Power, then, and how adoption of the development ethic makes it more accessible to our working lives as well as to society in general, will be the subject of Chapter 14, our final and summarizing chapter.

As always, let us begin our discussion by defining the importance of increased power to our working lives. We could say that three factors play a critical role in defining the degree of success enjoyed by any modern company. The *first*, and probably the least important due to the rapid dispersion of innovation throughout the industrial world, is the sophistication of technology available. The *second* critical factor is the extent to which worker potential and expertise at all levels of the hierarchy is utilized in getting the job done efficiently. The *third*, which, as we have said, is becoming increasingly important, is the company's ability to unleash and take advantage of its employees' creativity. Different cultures have different strengths in terms of these three factors. The strength of the United States, for example, has traditionally been in the areas of technology and creativity. More innovation, at least technological innovation, currently comes out of our country than any other. At the same time in recent history we have been one of if not *the* leading generator of new ideas, although in many instances we have not been the first to take advantage of them. Our weakness has been and remains our inability to effectively utilize employee potential and expertise.

The strengths of our competitors vary. The Japanese and other Asian nations are increasingly strong technologically. They also take much fuller advantage of their employees' productive potential than we do. In terms of creativity, however, Japanese corporations are better known for collecting and improving on other companies' new ideas than for coming up with their own.

European industrial powers are probably the best balanced in terms of our three criteria. They have kept pace technologically. At the same time, the movement to better utilize worker potential and expertise began in Europe. One of the first manifestations of this movement, the worker councils, appeared during the late 1940s when representatives of the workforce began sitting down with top-level management in such countries as Norway, France, Sweden, the Netherlands, and Germany to discuss and advise on a broad range of problems. More recently, the autonomous work groups of Volvo and other major corporations have become models for industries all over the world. In terms of creativity, the Industrial Revolution—the thing that started it all—was, again, largely the product of new technologies and management philosophy coming out of England, Germany, France, and other northern European countries. The steam engine, the loom, the locomotive, the machine tool industry, Adam Smith, and Herbert Spencer were all products of this part of the world and provided the foundations on which the revolution was built. In more recent times, creativity remains a cornerstone of the European industrial sector, although this sector no longer dominates the world scene the way it once did.

The current weakness of modern European powers is what has been labeled "creeping socialism." In many instances, corporations have been forced to put the interests of employees increasingly before those of the organization as a whole, rather than finding an appropriate balance. This tendency has affected the ability of firms to compete, at least in the world marketplace.

With the above general critique of the leading contenders in mind, then, one might say that the winner in terms of our current international economic competition is going to be the society that can correct its weakness the most rapidly. Such corrections, however, are not going to be easy, for what is involved in all three cases is serious cultural change. In terms of the United States, we must somehow get beyond the adversarial relationship that exerts so great an influence in our working environment. We must stop wasting so much of our collective energy on efforts to protect ourselves, on efforts to keep the other guy or gal from realizing his or her potential. We must, as we have said, truly adopt the team approach. The Asian peoples, in their turn, must find some way of moving beyond centuries of philosophical and religious conditioning that plays down individualism, that stresses fitting smoothly into society as opposed to striking out in a new direction, to "making waves," to wanting to be different. They must seek a better balance between these two abrasive but necessarily complementary extremes. Finally, our third grouping, the European nations, must move beyond, rather than retreat from, their socialist leanings and come up with something new, something that continues to provide the fundamental physical and emotional security generated by socialism but at the same time does not kill incentive and destroy individual initiative.

In terms of the ability of these three powers to make the necessary adjustment, I would say that the United States enjoys an advantage. Quite simply, our culture is not as old and inflexible as the others. We haven't had as long to become set in our ways. We are still capable of redefining and rebuilding our work life reality without too seriously rending its fabric, although a certain amount of trauma is obviously unavoidable. We have, in fact, already begun efforts at improvement in terms of our above-defined weakness. In earlier chapters I have mentioned several companies and corporations that are successfully instituting a positive team atmosphere. Now it is time to look more closely at these efforts in order to define exactly to what their success can be attributed.

Without reservation, my first observation along these lines is that all such efforts stem from management's desire to encourage employees to take a larger amount of responsibility for both their assigned duties and their output. In every instance, however, it has quickly become obvious that employees are more willing to accept increased responsibility if it is coupled with increasing amounts of authority, at least in their own area of expertise. This realization, of course, involves the issue of power, of every employee's natural desire for growing amounts of control over things affecting his or her working life and developmental efforts. Power, then, the theme of this chapter, eventually and inevitably has become the crux of all team-building efforts. Participants in such efforts have been forced to ask where the power currently lies, and, more important, where it should lie in order to best facilitate the realization of corporate objectives.

The answers to this last question by this time ought to be obvious. The concept involved is a simple and well-proven one. The major problem faced, therefore, is not generally a problem of understanding. Rather, it is one of implementation. Foremen, supervisors, superintendents, directors, vice presidents, and presidents have worked hard, fought hard, and made a lot of personal sacrifices to get where they are. Because of this history, the tendency when they reach a higher level is to immediately suck decision-making authority inward, to take it away from subordinates. The new manager on all levels does this to both prove and protect him- or herself. He or she is vulnerable and can't afford any mistakes. The popular logic, therefore, is that the fewer decisions others are permitted to make, the less chance there is for a mistake. Also, of course, the new manager isn't quite sure of how he or she is going to handle these new responsibilities. The manager might, indeed, want to try some innovative things but at the same time needs to keep tight control of the situation. Finally, the new manager would like to trust his or her reports, but is afraid to. The road upward has been too rough. Some of these reports obviously would not be against helping to make him or her look bad.

My second observation has to do with that which is most necessary if corporate efforts to further diffuse power are, indeed, to succeed. No matter how much time, energy, and money is spent attempting to change the above-defined culture of defensiveness, nothing is going to happen until the highest authority, usually a president or CEO, truly understands and is committed to the necessary process. This observation, as I have said earlier, almost by definition rules out success when a leader's skills are mainly political. Even when they are technical, however, and in some cases when they are cultural, success is by no means assured. The president's sudden realization, after months of relatively smooth sailing, that decision-making authority must, indeed, be diffused at top levels as well if the desired change is

to be achieved can stop a project dead. The leader is the key. Everyone, and I mean *everyone*, has one eye on that person. Any hesita-
tion, any sign of reluctance, any suspected loss of interest can trigger
a very abrupt return to the status quo. Until those facilitating the
process, therefore, are absolutely sure that the president or CEO
understands the ways in which a further dispersion of power will
benefit his or her career and personal development as well as that of
subordinates, they should proceed with extreme caution.

The third and final observation that I would make has to do with
middle-level management—with superintendents, supervisors, and foremen, to be specific. Some experts consider one or more of the levels
involved to be in danger of becoming extinct. Traditionally, middle
managers have been part of the problem-solving and decision-making
hierarchy on the "nuts and bolts" or operational side of the business.
They have been deeply involved in getting the daily quota of widgets
or thingamabobs out the door on schedule. What an increasing
number of corporations are saying now, however, is that so many
levels of input are not necessary. They are saying that if hourly
workers can, indeed, solve their own problems, and should, indeed,
enjoy more power, or control, over their part of the process, the time
has come for a layer or two of management to disappear.

As a result of this trend, several things are happening. One, which
is obvious, is that while developmental opportunities for lower-level
workers are increasing, those for supervisory-level employees are
being dealt a severe and often fatal blow. Another is that middle-level
managers are rapidly developing a reputation for being reactionary,
for being the most defensive of all. They are considered the major
roadblock to progress, the ones who are going to require the most
effort to convert, the ones who either directly or indirectly will do
everything possible to scuttle attempts at innovation. Another thing
that is happening, and perhaps the most critical in terms of our argument, is that in dissolving a layer or two of middle management,
companies are losing valuable experience and expertise that has been
years and years in the making. They are throwing out one of the most
valuable ingredients for success. They are rushing too quickly to
judgement without paying adequate attention to possible alternatives.

Adoption of the development ethic, in my mind, will facilitate the
generation of more healthy and productive attitudes and alternatives
at all the levels of management mentioned in my above observations.
Starting with the top level, that of president or CEO, leaders who

have not devoted their entire lives to the pursuit of plenty, who have a much richer background, will tend not to be so dictatorial. They will not encourage or accept a work atmosphere where power politics prevail, where nobody, including themselves, is to be trusted. One of the steps they will take in order to create this more comfortable, productive environment will be to favor direct reports and other employees who demonstrate a more comprehensive perspective, who are interested in improving their overall quality of life rather than simply in beating everyone in sight like our friend from Chapter 5. They will surround themselves with people who have realized that while advancement is important, peer relationships are just as important or even more important, and that a well-planned and coordinated team approach is the best way to achieve corporate as well as individual objectives.

Concerning our dire predictions for middle management, the development ethic again should help define a less destructive and more profitable alternative. We have said that once technology begins doing increasing amounts of the repetitious "grunt" work, employees on all levels will be freed for more challenging, creative efforts. One class of such efforts will be research and development. Part of any holistic research and development program, to my mind, centers around the continuing attempt to improve an organization's design in terms of both technical and management systems. In the new world workplace, therefore, at the same time that daily operational decisions are being made a parallel set of nontraditional systems-improvement projects and decisions will be materializing.

"All right," I hear. "That makes sense. We can all think of ways to improve the way things are done. But who has the time? Who is going to organize such efforts? Who is going to take responsibility for keeping them moving?" Ah, yes, who, indeed, will have the time, the necessary experience, and the management skills required to put together and run such efforts? My obvious reply is that the middle managers should do it, some of those people now threatened with obsolescence. Such a setup would reduce their role in the operational decision-making cycle, thus shortening it. It would simultaneously, however, present them with new challenges that they, out of all candidates, are best equipped to meet. I have *never* shared drinks with an old-time supervisor or even a young one and not eventually heard, "Well, I'll tell you one thing. I have a lot of respect for Mr. Smith, but if *I* was running this show, I sure as hell would make some changes. People are doing some of the *stupidest* things, and nobody seems to care, or even to notice."

In effect, then, under the new system, supervisors would function more as internal consultants. They would lead and coordinate change efforts rather than fearing and trying to block them. The type of power they'd exercise in this new situation obviously would be different and not as direct as that which they now enjoy. But it would, in the final analysis, probably also be much more rewarding to both themselves and to the company.

In terms of our second major area of concern—society as a whole—power is perhaps the most important issue. Politically, the people of the United States enjoy probably as much or more of it than the people of any other nation in history. Our Constitution and system of government have helped assure that. Yet, as we all know, we frequently do not accept the responsibility involved. We take an awful lot for granted, placing support of our power-generating institutions low on our list of priorities. Adoption of the development ethic should help us understand more clearly the dangers inherent in this type of thinking. The critical role of power and of how it is diffused in any healthy society will become more obvious when we begin enjoying increasing amounts of control over our time and resources. Also, as we start to develop a more balanced perspective in terms of both our individual and societal potential, we will realize the key role that power plays in achieving the desired integration of activities, as well as in gaining the desired access to those inputs necessary to our efforts. The on-going quest for satisfactory amounts of power, therefore, will become an integral part of our lives, just as will the on-going quest for satisfactory amounts of plenty, truth, good, and beauty.

Another critical area where we seem to fall short and where our attitude toward power seems ambivalent is in the formulation of our foreign policy. The conflict ethic, the combativeness, and the paranoia that have traditionally hampered our industrial efforts are also in evidence here. In some instances it seems as though we actually choose to make enemies out of potential allies rather than taking those steps that would encourage cooperation, just like corporate divisions and departments choose to make enemies out of each other rather than seeking to bridge the gaps that separate. We see the fact that another nation has a perspective different from ours as a threat, or some politician, who depends on "the politics of fear" to rally support, makes it into a threat.

We are, of course, not unique in this. The above-defined mentality, in fact, seems to be increasingly popular in many parts of the world. The targets vary, covering a wide range of political and philosophical opponents. In the case of the United States, of course, the main culprit, our major adversary, the primary enemy that our policy is focused on defeating is communism. We feel that we are justified in doing whatever is necessary to prevent its spread, and because we are locked into the conflict mentality our tools for achieving this end are more often than not the tools of war and violence. But what, again, is this demon "communism"? What makes it so threatening? Communism is basically a system for distributing the wealth produced by a society, a system that in the long run doesn't work because it kills incentive. Communism also depends on centralized economic control, which again in the long run doesn't work because it can't pay adequate attention to local variations that make the difference.

But what about the short run? What does it provide in the short run? What has accounted for its many followers? Countries have become communist in two ways. The first is through internal revolution. The second is through invasion and subjugation. In terms of the first, it has cropped up in countries—the Soviet Union, China, Cuba, Nicaragua—where the existing plenty was poorly distributed. Before communism, two classes existed in these countries. One was an extremely small upper-class that controlled the government and economy, manipulating both to satisfy its own desires. The other, larger part of the population was made up of peasants and urban laborers, of people locked into slave or, at best, subsistence-level work with little chance of improving their situation.

In each one of the above instances, then, communism was adopted, at least initially, as a means of facilitating redistribution of the wealth so that a greater percentage of the population could enjoy a greater degree of both physical and emotional security. Most of the people who helped bring communist governments to power in these countries, we must remember, were not political philosophers or political radicals. Rather, they were common folk whose main concern was finding enough plenty to survive on. Communism promised them this amount of plenty, and, more important, began delivering on its promise almost immediately. Dictators still ran things, but this new breed of dictators was different in that it demonstrated as well as preached concern. Freedom was still limited, but, at the same time, food became available, medical attention was provided where none had existed before, and adults gained educational opportunity, not only for their children, but for themselves as well.

What is critical to our discussion, however, is what begins to happen in such countries once communism matures and once the people start taking for granted continuing access to the basics of survival. Based on our framework of the various types of work through which people progress on their way to holistic development, it is obvious that at this point they begin seeking ways to further improve their situation—ways to earn more money and gain more comfort, opportunity, and pleasure from life. It is also obvious that at this point, as we have indicated, the weaknesses of the system begin to appear, thus precipitating a shift toward free enterprise as a means of increasing access to the other key developmental inputs.

In terms of economically underdeveloped countries, then, we can actually visualize communism and democracy as being part of the same continuum. One leads naturally into the other. The desire of many of our leaders in the United States, of course, is to have these countries skip the communism stage and jump right to democracy and capitalism. Such a direct transition, however, as history has shown, can be very difficult. For one thing, the mass education essential to our political and economic way of life does not exist. For another, peoples of underdeveloped nations are accustomed to being dominated so that the rise of a strongman is harder to stave off. As a result of these vulnerabilities a sham democracy, rather than the real thing, frequently emerges, as it did in the Philippines under Marcos and in various Latin American and African countries. Dissidence is controlled and the elite remain in power, simply mouthing a slightly different line in order to gain international acceptance. In actuality, however, the wealth has not been redistributed, life has not really improved for the majority of the population, and the true potential of the country has not been released.

The question that must be addressed at this point is, "Why, exactly, are we so afraid of communism?" The ends sought ideally— improvement of the individual and societal situation—are certainly no different from those sought by democracies. The means used to at least begin achieving these ends are, indeed, different. But this shouldn't bother us because, as we have said, it is becoming increasingly obvious that, in the long run at least, our system is much more effective in all areas of concern. The real problem, it turns out, is not so much one of communism as an economic and social philosophy.

Rather, the thing we fear is, in actuality, the tendency of certain communist nations—the USSR, Cuba, and Vietnam in our time—not to wait for Marx's prophesied world domination to occur as a result of unavoidable economic evolution, but to attempt to hasten the process through force of arms and subversion.

Largely as a result of this well-founded fear, but also as a result of our no longer well-founded conflict mentality that compounds the fear and frequently exacerbates the problem, we miss opportunities and continue to fight economic progress in communist nations even when the people have expressed a desire to begin shifting more in our direction. I find it interesting that the communist country we have interfered with the least in terms of its political and economic evolution is the one that has moved the most rapidly toward free enterprise. I am referring, of course, to China. The shift we are witnessing there is the result of many variables. A key one, for example, is the pragmatic nature of the Asian peoples. But I continue to suspect that the fact we have not been able to seriously disrupt its efforts at reorientation due to the physical distance separating us, the lack of cultural understanding, or whatever, has proven beneficial.

On the other hand, I recently spoke to a French friend who had just returned from a trip through the Soviet Union. He talked about how visitors there can get so much more for their dollars and francs on the street than through official money-changing channels. Then he said, "But it doesn't make any difference, really, all those rubles. The problem is that there's still nothing to buy, nothing at all, except maybe good vodka. I was there six years ago. Things haven't changed one bit since then that I can see. Everyone's fed up with the situation."

When I hear things like this, it's hard for me to believe that an opportunity doesn't exist for a greater number of positive inroads to be made with the Soviet Union through economic initiatives. It's hard for me to believe that if we unraveled ourselves a bit from the massive web of intrigue and power politics we are currently bound up in with this opponent and took another look, this option would not begin to make increasing amounts of sense.

Concerning new communist countries, our inability to differentiate clearly between the evolutionary and expansionist faces of this doctrine again muddles our judgement. Our policy, fairly obviously, is to force them to do our bidding, despite the fact that the change to communism was supported by a majority of the people. Our efforts thus far in such situations, mainly for this reason, have met with limited success. The peasants might grow a little hungrier due to our sanctions and embargoes, but they are used to being hungry. Besides, they now have something new—their nationalistic fervor—to help sustain them. The main thing that such a posture brings, in many instances, is ridicule from a growing number of our friends as well as our enemies.

It seems, then, that the results of our foreign policy frequently have been opposite to what we desired. Rather than moving the people of Third World countries away from communism, we have sometimes pushed them closer to it, encouraging ties they might not necessarily have wanted. Worse than that, however, is the fact that our actions have put us into the same category as the more aggressive communist nations. People in many Third World countries are still at step one. They are trying to discover ways to distribute more equitably the existing plenty and to generate enough new plenty to provide everyone with the basics. They have chosen the system they think will facilitate this process most readily, but we won't accept their reasoning. In other words, in terms of economic policy at least, we are just as unwilling as the more aggressive communist nations to wait and let evolution prove us right. We are just as unwilling to show the people of Nicaragua, for example, the respect that they are now struggling to gain. We are just as unwilling to allow them to exercise the control that we have defined as the key to individual and societal development.

Once again, when we enter the new world and adopt the new ethic our emphasis as a society should begin shifting. As a result of this shift both of the above scenarios should change. Concerning mature communist nations, we will realize that the best way to blunt their threat is to help make the lives of their people richer and fuller. Someone who has been able to steadily improve his or her situation is far less willing to risk what he or she had gained than someone still living on the edge of poverty. People whose development is well-balanced and full hold far less respect for violence than those who continue to be trapped in the struggle for plenty. This strategy is not new. Historically, it has been introduced by a variety of governments in a variety of situations. The post-World War II Marshall Plan is a modern day example of its use.

Concerning new communist nations such as Nicaragua, instead of giving them just two alternatives to choose from, their way or ours, a third will be introduced. Because our primary objective will be the realization of positive human potential on a world as well as national scale we will say, "Okay, you've had it rough and now you've picked communism as at least the first step in your rebuilding effort. We'll respect that choice because we respect you and believe that your ultimate objective is no different from ours. At the same time, however, we want to make clear that in the long run we think free enterprise will eventually prove the better means to your desired ends. In fact, in order to demonstrate the strength of our belief, as well as our good intentions, we are going to use our economic power to help you generate the plenty necessary to meet your primary needs. After that's out of the way, we'll see what happens. Just one thing. Don't go trying to force your new way of life on your neighbors. We respect your right to pick the best path to development. You, in turn, must respect theirs. If you're going to woo them, we suggest strongly that you do it by example, not by intimidation."

With this approach, instead of a "win-lose" situation, there will be a greater chance of creating a "win-win" situation. On the one hand the population involved will achieve the desired foundational inputs much more rapidly. At the same time, the United States will be seen as a friend and, in a relatively short period, as a model to emulate in terms of more holistic development. One of the questions this latter alternative raises, however, as do all alternatives of this nature, is, "How do we finance such an effort? Equipment and expertise cost money. We know that from our own domestic development efforts, which consume the largest chunk of our tax revenues. How, then, do we cover the price tag when we get involved on a world scale?"

One part of the answer to the above question is that such projects won't be as expensive as we might presume. First, because of our evolving ethic, corporations and individuals will be more willing to volunteer their time, expertise, and equipment, thus cutting costs. Second, with the corporate world more deeply involved, we will probably succeed in eliminating much of the bureaucratic waste and the corruption usually found in foreign aid efforts.

Another part of the answer is that as our developmental expenditures increase, our military expenditures should decrease. From a developmental point of view, the monies being poured into armaments are largely wasted anyhow. Except for some of the research that might spawn peaceful applications, there is little or no return on investment. We, of course, have to protect ourselves against increasing amounts of terrorism as well as from those who would force their political, religious, or economic views on us. I suspect, however, that in the long run the best way of doing this is by addressing the developmental problems of the world rather than by arming it to the teeth.

In sum, then, little doubt remains in a growing number of minds that at this point in history a change in our perspective and a redefinition of our reality is the most viable alternative in terms of our foreign policy. The old ways don't work anymore. As lethal as swords, guns, or conventional bombs have been, they don't threaten the survival of humanity and of all life on earth the way that our newest generation of weapons do. According to experts like Carl Sagan, there is no real defense. No matter how elaborate, no matter how sophisticated our precautions might be, something or someone is going to get through, and that something or someone will probably be more than enough to finish us off.

Just as the previously discussed computer is changing the rules of our working and leisure lives, then, these new weapons are changing the rules by which we must negotiate our cultural and national disagreements. The old definitions upon which we have built our security are no longer valid. A new set must be agreed upon, and quickly, before human misjudgement and fear make modern science and technology a threat, rather than a blessing, once too often.

But how do we begin this process? How do we set about redefining our foreign policy? The first and most critical step, in my mind, is the generation of a universally accepted standard concerning the ways in which power can and should be used. Such a task might sound extremely difficult, even impossible. But it is not, for with the development ethic we have the starting point that we need. According to our new world mentality, quite simply, the legitimate uses of power include all those that enable people to gain the plenty, truth, good, and beauty necessary to the realization of their potential without, at the same time, depriving others of these same inputs. This standard, in effect, makes our ideological struggles much less convoluted by focusing more on desirable ends than on the means used to achieve them. It clears the ideological battlefield of all but two groups of contestants, the first includes all those who support human development for others as well as themselves, no matter what vehicle for change they choose; the second includes all those whose objective is to subvert development for others by denying access to the necessary inputs, no matter what rationalization they might offer.

And that's it, that's about all I have to say, except that in closing there is one concept I would like to return to briefly. I want to return because it is a concept I have introduced continually when talking about development, and because it is the concept that, perhaps more than any other, exemplifies what this book has been about. It is, as you might guess, the concept of potential, the human potential that developmental activities help us to realize.

If I were asked to expound on what life is all about, part of my answer according to what I have said in *Work and Rewards* would be that it centers on our attempts to realize our many types of potential in order to gain the desired respect. Scientists, for example, talk about the fact that we presently use only a very small portion of our brains. They enjoy speculating on the prodigious feats we would be capable of if we could do better. I'm sure many of us feel the same way about overall human potential. It boggles my partially developed mind to think about what we could accomplish if every single human being on this earth realized at least a good percentage of his or hers. The results would be absolutely awesome.

To me, then, this is *the* challenge lying before us, the one to which modern man should begin paying the most attention. Everything else pales beside it. Also, it is my belief that if we *did* begin concentrating our energies and resources on this challenge, on making better use of our physical, intellectual, emotional, and spiritual potential, most of the other problems currently competing for attention would disappear in fairly rapid order. Many of them, like war, would cease to make sense, while development-related ones would be much easier to define and attack.

As a free society we create our own reality. We mustn't let anyone tell us differently. Because we create our own reality, we can also modify it. All that it takes to set off the desired change process is the necessary new definitions and the necessary degree of commitment. We now, hopefully, have a start on the definitions. At the same time, commitment to positive change is inherent in healthy individuals and societies. It is time, then, that we begin moving more rapidly toward the new world that now is truly within our reach.

BIBLIOGRAPHY

Ackoff, Russell L. *Creating the Corporate Future.* New York: Wiley, 1981.
———. "Does Quality of Life Have to Be Quantified?" *General Systems* 20, 1975.
———. *Management in Small Doses.* New York: Wiley, 1986.
———. *Redesigning the Future.* New York: Wiley, 1974.
———. "The Mismatch Between Educational Systems and the Requirements for Successful Management." *Wharton Alumni Magazine*, Spring 1986.
———. "Toward a System of Systems Concepts." *Management Science* 3, 11: 1971.
Ackoff, Russell L., and C. West Churchman. *Methods of Inquiry: An Introduction to Philosophy and Scientific Method.* Saint Louis: Educational Publishers, 1950.
Ackoff, Russell L., and Fred E. Emery. *On Purposeful Systems.* New York: Aldine Atherton, 1972.
Ackoff, Russell L., and J. Gharajedaghi. *Prologue to National Development Planning.* New York: Greenwood, 1986.
Adler, Mortimer. *Aristotle for Everyone: Difficult Thought Made Easy.* New York: McMillan, 1978.
Allen, Kerry, Isolda Chaplin, Shirley Keller, and Donna Hill. *Volunteers From the Workplace.* Washington, DC: National Center of Voluntary Action, 1979.
Allio, Robert J. "Executive Retraining: The Obsolete MBA." *Business and Society Review*, Summer 1984.
"America's Business Schools: Priorities for Change: A Report by the Business-Higher Education Forum." Washington, DC, May 1985.

Avedisian, Joyce, Ron Cowin, Doug Ferguson, and Bill Roth. "Beyond Crisis Management." *Pulp and Paper International*, February 1986.

Axinn, June, and Herman Levin. *Social Welfare: A History of American Response to Need.* New York: Dodd, Mead, 1975.

Bannister, Robert C. *Social Darwinism: Science and Myth.* Philadelphia: Temple Univ. Press, 1978.

Barnes, Norman. "Rethinking Corporate Charity." *Fortune*, October 1974.

Batter, William M. "Productivity and the Working Environment." The Wharton School of the University of Pennsylvania Lecture Series.

Boriako, Allen. "The Chip." *National Geographic* 162, 4: October 1982.

Brom, Thomas. "The Parttime Job: A New Way of Life." Philadelphia *Bulletin*, December 3, 1978.

Capaldi, Nicholas, ed. *The Enlightenment: The Proper Study of Mankind.* New York: Putnam's Sons, 1967.

Cardwell, D. S. L. *Turning Points in Western Technology.* New York: Neale Watson Academic Publications, 1972.

Chems, Albert, and Louis Davis. *The Quality of Working Life.* Vols. 1, 2. London: Collier Macmillan, 1973.

Commoner, Barry. *The Closing Circle.* New York: Alfred A. Knopf, 1971.

"Company's Courses Go Collegiate." *Business Week*, February 26, 1979.

Cooper, Michael, Peter Gelfond, and Patricia Foley. "Early Warning Signals—Growing Discontent Among Managers." *Business*, January-February 1980.

"Crysler Ties Executive Bonuses to Worker Profit-Sharing." *Los Angeles Times*, April 19, 1988.

Cutterbuck, David. "The Future of Work." *International Management*, August 1979.

Dembart, Lee. "Expert Computers Raising Questions." *Philadelphia Inquirer*, Sunday, December 12, 1982.

"Developing Managers Not a Corporate Priority." *The Wall Street Journal*, April 18, 1988.

Dickson, John. "Plight of Middle Management." *Management Today*, December 1977.

Durant, Will. *The Reformation.* New York: Simon and Schuster, 1957.

Ellul, Jacques. *The Technological Society.* New York: Vintage, 1967.

Emery, Fred. *Futures We Are In.* Leiden, the Netherlands: Martinus Nijhoff Social Sciences Division, 1977.

——— . "The Fifth Wave? Embarking on the Next Forty Years." Unpublished manuscript, May 1978.

Emery, Fred, and Einar Thorsrud. *Democracy at Work.* Leiden, the Netherlands: Martinus Nijhoff Social Sciences Division, 1976.

Engang, Robert. *The Renaissance.* London: D. Van Norstrand, 1967.

Fenwick, P., and E. Lawler. "What You Really Want from Your Job." *Psychology Today*, May 1978.

Freeman, Alix. "Behind Every Successful Robot is a Technician." *Careers*, 1983.

Friedmann, John. *Retracking America: A Theory of Transactive Planning.* New York: Anchor, 1973.

Friedman, Milton. *Tax Limitation, Inflation, and the Role of Government.* Dallas: The Fisher Institute, 1978.

Galbraith, John K. "When Work Isn't Work." *Parade* Sunday Supplement Magazine, *The Morning Call*, Allentown, PA, February 10, 1985.

Gay, Peter. *The Enlightenment: A Comparative Analogy.* New York: Simon and Schuster, 1973.

George, Claude. *The History of Management Thought.* Englewood Cliffs, NJ: Prentice-Hall, 1968.

Gharajedaghi, Jamshid. "On the Nature of Development." *Human Systems Management* 4: 1984.

———. "Obstructions to Development." *Human Systems Management* 4: 1984.

———. *Toward a Systems Theory of Organization.* Seaside, CA: Intersystems Publications, 1985.

Gilman, Robert. "Job Sharing Is Good." *The Co-Evolutionary Quarterly*, Spring 1978.

Ginzberg, Eli. "The Mechanization of Work." *Scientific American*, September 1982.

Guiliano, Vincent. "The Mechanization of Office Work." *Scientific American*, September 1982.

Gunn, Thomas. "The Mechanization of Design and Manufacturing." *Scientific American*, September 1982.

Hackman, J. Richard, and J. Lloyd Suttle. *Improving Life at Work.* Santa Monica, CA: Goodyear, 1977.

Han, Frank H. *Money and Inflation.* Cambridge, MA: MIT Press, 1981.

Harrison, John B., and Richard E. Sullivan. *A Short History of Western Civilization.* New York: Alfred A. Knopf, 1960.

Harvard Business School MBA Program 1988. Cambridge, MA: Harvard Univ., 1988.

Herzberg, Frederick. "Work and the Nature of Man." *World*, 1966.

Hodgson, Richard. "The Death and Resurrection of Management Teams." *The Business Quarterly*, Winter 1974.

Hofstadter, Richard. *Social Darwinism In American Thought.* New York: George Braziller, 1959.

Holden, Constance. "Innovation: Japan Races Ahead as U.S. Falters." *Science*, November 14, 1980.

Huddleston, Kenneth, and Dorothy Fenwick. "The Productivity Challenge: Business/Education Partnership." *Training and Development Journal* 37, 4: April 1983.

Hymowitz, Carol. "Employers Take Over Where Schools Fail to Teach the Basics." *Wall Street Journal*, January 22, 1981.

Iacocca, Lee A., with William Novak. *Iacocca: An Autobiography*. New York: Bantam, 1984.

"Industry Must Automate, Emigrate, or Evaporate," *U.S. News and World Report*, January 16, 1984.

Japan, Government of, Ministry of International Trade and Industry. "The Vision of MITI Policies in the 1980s." Tokyo: MITI, 1980.

Jardim, Anne. *The First Henry Ford: A Study in Personality and Business Leadership*. Cambridge, MA: MIT Press, 1970.

Jenkins, David. *Job Power*. Baltimore: Penguin, 1973.

Jenkins, Roger L., Richard C. Reisenstein, and F. G. Rogers. "Report Card on the MBA." *Harvard Business Review*, September-October 1984.

Johnson and Johnson. *Employee Development Review Guidebook*. New Brunswick, N.J., 1978.

Johnson and Johnson. *New Manager Transition: A Management Tool*. New Brunswick, N.J., 1981.

Johnston, Joseph, and Associates. *Educating Managers*. San Francisco: Jossey-Bass, 1986.

Kerr, Clark, and Jerome Rosow, eds. *Work In America: The Decade Ahead*. New York: Van Nostrand Reinhold, 1979.

Klemm, Frederick. *A History of Western Technology*. Cambridge, MA: MIT Press, 1954.

Lerner, Max, ed. *The Portable Veblen*. New York: Viking, 1948.

Leontief, Wassily. "The Distribution of Work and Income." *Scientific American*, September 1982.

Levitan, Sar A., and William B. Johnston. *Work Is Here To Stay, Alas*. Salt Lake City, UT: Olympus, 1973.

Lohr, Steve. "Overhauling America's Business Management." *New York Times Magazine*, January 4, 1981.

"Managing, A Study in Neglect." *Los Angeles Times*, May 23, 1988.

Mayer, Martin. *Madison Avenue, USA*. New York: Harper, 1958.

McNeil Pharmaceutical. *Performance, Potential, and Development Review Guidebook*. Spring House, PA, 1983.

Michaels, Marguerite. "A Report Card From Our Teachers." *Parade* Sunday Supplement, *The Morning Call*, Allentown, PA, December 1, 1985.

"More Companies Let Workers Set Up Shop at Home," *The Orange County Register*, July 13, 1986.

Naisbitt, John. *Megatrends*. New York: Werner Books, 1982.

"New Breed of Workers." *U.S. News and World Report*, September 3, 1979.

Perelman, Lewis J. "The Future of Learning: The Age of School Is Over." *Orange County Register*. Santa Ana, CA: March 30, 1986.

Rader, Dotson. "Why Children Run Away." *Parade* Sunday Supplement, *The Morning Call*, Allentown, PA, August 18, 1985.

"Rebuilding America: Start at the Factory." *Wall Street Journal*, May 16, 1988.

Reich, Charles. *The Greening of America.* New York: Random House, 1970.

"Remaking the Harvard MBA." *Business Week*, March 24, 1986.

Roth, William. "Comparing the Effects of Cooperation, Competition, and Conflict on the Speed with Which Different Personality Types and Personality Type Pairs Can Generate Useful Solutions to Problems." Ph.D. dissertation, University of Pennsylvania.

————. "Designing a New Academic Management Training Program." *SAM Advanced Management Journal*, Winter 1988.

————. *Problem Solving for Managers.* New York: Praeger, 1985.

————. "What's Going On Down In Louisiana?" *Pulp and Paper International*, September 1987.

Sagan, Carl. "Star Wars: The Leaky Shield." *Parade* Sunday Supplement, *The Morning Call*, Allentown, PA, December 8, 1985.

Schon, Donald. *Beyond the Stable State.* London: Temple Smith, 1971.

Simonetta, Joseph. *Russell, Alexandra and John.* Los Angeles: Simonetta, 1981.

————. *The Heroes Are Us.* Los Angeles: Simonetta, 1984.

"Some Lessons for the Decade Ahead: A New Hand in the Workplace—The Robot." *U.S. News and World Report*, January 21, 1980.

Taylor, Frederick. *The Principles of Scientific Management.* New York: Harper, 1911.

The Wharton School MBA Program Bulletin, 1988–89, Philadelphia, PA.

Tichy, Noel. *Managing Strategic Change.* New York: Wiley Interscience, 1983.

Toffler, Alvin. *Future Shock.* New York: Random House, 1970.

Trist, Eric. "The Evolution of Socio-Technical Systems." *Issues in the Quality of Working Life.* No. 2. Ontario: Ontario Ministry of Labor, 1980.

————. "The Quality of Working Life and Organizational Improvement." Unpublished manuscript. Management and Behavioral Science Center, The Wharton School, Philadelphia, PA, October 1979.

Trist, Eric, G. W. Higgins, H. Murray, and A. B. Pollock. *Organizational Choice.* London: Tavistock Institute Publications, 1963.

Veblen, Thorstein B. *The Theory of the Leisure Class: An Economic Study of Institutions.* New York: Random, 1934.

Von Martin, Alfred. "Sociology of the Renaissance." In *The Renaissance*, Karl H. Dannenfeldt, ed. Boston: D. C. Heath, 1956.

Weber, Eugene. *The Western Tradition from the Renaissance to the Atomic Age.* Los Angeles: D. C. Heath, 1965.

Wells, H. G. *The Outline of History.* Garden City, NY: Garden City Books, 1949.

"When Companies Tell Business Schools What To Teach." *Business Week*, February 10, 1986.

INDEX

ABOUT THE AUTHOR

WILLIAM F. ROTH, JR., is a graduate of Dartmouth College and the University of Pennsylvania. He received his Ph.D. in management sciences from the Wharton School in 1982. Currently he is an associate professor at Moravian College and senior partner of Roth & Associates, a consulting firm that works with corporate quality improvement efforts. Recently he was asked to act as advisor to a congressional task force designing a nationwide community-based quality education and improvement effort. He has previously worked as manager of organization design with the International Paper Company and as an assistant professor at LaSalle University.